Indian Life in Town and Country

Indian Life in Town and Country

HERBERT COMPTON

GYAN

Published by

Gyan Publishing House
5, Ansari Road
Daryaganj, New Delhi-110002
Phone: 011-47034999, 9811692060
E-mail: books@gyanbooks.com

Distribution Network
gyanbooks.com
India, USA, Canada, UK, Australia, France

ISBN: 978-81-212-8770-8 (PB)
First Published, 1904

2nd Impression 2023

Printed at: Gyan Press, Delhi.

Indian Life in Town and Country
Author: Herbert Compton

INDIAN LIFE IN TOWN AND COUNTRY

Indian Life in Town and Country

BY

HERBERT COMPTON

Author of "A Free Lance in a Far Land," "A King's Hussar," etc.

PUBLISHED FOR THE

BAY VIEW READING CLUB

CENTRAL OFFICE: BOSTON BOULEVARD

DETROIT, MICH.

BY G. P. PUTNAM'S SONS

NEW YORK LONDON

CONTENTS

Native Indian Life

Contents

NATIVE INDIAN LIFE

INDIAN LIFE IN TOWN AND COUNTRY

CHAPTER I

INDIA AS IT IS

IT is a habit of current speech to refer to India much as one does to France, Spain, or Germany, conscious only that it is a far more extensive country. In the map of the world, it is depicted as an all-red possession, which tends to the suggestion of a homogeneous land. But it is, in fact, a conglomeration of distinct kingdoms and peoples, differing as widely in conditions and characteristics as Russia and Portugal, or the Norwegian and the Turk.

The term "Indian" should convey to the mind the same cosmopolitan suggestion as the expression "European." Under this really generic designation are grouped numerous races as distinct and individual as the Frenchman and the German, the Dutchman and the Greek. And when we come to discuss "Our Neighbour the Indian," it must be understood we are arbitrarily making concrete what is in the abstract a heterogeneous, polyglot combination of individuals, who belong to a dozen different nationalities, speak a Babel of tongues, and live in a variety of countries, the physical features of which differ as much as their climatic conditions.

If we can suppose ourselves in the position of a Cossack riding through the Khyber Pass, and cantering down to Calcutta, Cape Comorin, and Karachi, we shall be able to get the best idea of the races who inhabit India in their appropriate distribution and sequence, and observe them toning off like a chromatic scale. Our Cossack will find them as diverse as if he penetrated from Moscow to Sweden, Spain, and Greece. As he emerges from the rugged Pass which has been the principal gateway of invasion, he will be confronted with bearded Mahomedans, speaking Pushto; and stalwart Sikhs, speaking Punjabi, who will gaze at the intruder with the calm confidence begotten of broad shoulders, brawny muscles, and a stature often exceeding six feet. Penetrating farther, he will observe but little deterioration in the clean-run men of Rohilkhund and Oudh, the hardy Jat cultivators about Delhi, the martial Rajpoots of Rajputana, and the hardy Baluchis of the Indus Valley (all speaking strange tongues), as they rise in his path in the segment of a circle which stretches from mid-Himalayas to mid-Sind. These races will coincide physically with the Northern peoples of Europe, the Scandinavian, Saxon, Celt, and Teuton. Their origin is Aryan, Scythian, Arab, and Tartar.

Pursuing his road east, south-east, and south, the Cossack will discover in the inhabitants of Lower Sind, Kattywar, Guzerat, the Northern Deccan, Central India, and the Upper Gangetic Valley, races somewhat smaller in stature and darker in complexion (speaking several new languages), who may not be inaptly compared to the French, the Slavs, and the Hungarians. The next radius of the circle brings us to the coastal countries, where dwell the effeminate Bengalis, the midget races who inhabit the Malabar seaboard, and the Tamil and Talugu speaking folk of Southern India. These, and the Burmese in the Far East, may fitly represent the Mediterranean nationalities of Europe. They spring from Dravidian and Mongolian stock, and the infusion of Aryan with non-Aryan blood. The scale of physical development is distinctly a sliding one, as it drops down the peninsula, the comparative giants of the north melting into the middle-sized Indo-Mongolians of the Far East, and the Dravidian dwarfs of the extreme south. Here and there, chiefly in mountain or desert tracts, aboriginal races will have been met, belonging to the Kolarian division, and displaying characteristics of their own. If you could muster a representative assemblage of all these races, you would find that they expressed themselves in over seventy different tongues, represented every shade of complexion, and every degree of physical development, and displayed far greater divergencies than a similar gathering from Continental Europe could produce.

In similar wise, our roving Cossack will have passed through as many countries as there are races. On his entry into India, Cashmere, on his left, will have supplied a standard of terrestrial perfection. It is the Riviera of our Eastern Empire, where, in the past, the Mogul Emperors were wont to revel, and where, in the present, the fortunate Anglo-Indian flits when he desires to enjoy a supreme holiday. Radiating east and south, the Cossack will perceive in the snowy slopes and cool valleys of the Himalayas, the sub-montane districts below them, the level plains of the Punjab, the stifling sands of Sind, the arid deserts of Rajputana, the steaming valley of the Gangetic basin, the rugged highlands of Central India, the tableland of the Deccan, the garden province of Guzerat, the palm-fringed Malabar coast, the paddy-fields of Burmah, the rocky *hinterlands* of the interior of Southern India, the fertile coastal territories of the Coromandel, the forested tracts of the Ghauts, Mysore, and the Wynaad, the rolling downs of the Neilgherries, and the tropic glories of Travancore—he will recognise in all these varying scenes distinct countries, differing one from another in aspect and altitude, in flora and fauna, and in soil and climate, as completely as do the peoples who inhabit them in race, religion, and language.

Meanwhile, our hardy traveller might have experienced vicissitudes of temperature and rainfall able to confound all his previous knowledge, even if it comprehended a winter on the shores of the Baltic, and a summer on those of the Black Sea. For instance, at Murree, in the Punjab, a hill station within a few hours of the Indian Aldershot, he might have been buried in six feet of snow; at Cheerapoonji, in Assam, half-drowned in a rainfall that exceeds four hundred inches a year. The process of thawing could have been accelerated by a trip to Jacobabad in Sind, where the thermometer looks down at 130 degrees in the shade; and for a dry climate Bickaneer is hard to beat, seeing that twenty-four months may pass without any rain at all. Incidentally, our enterprising Cossack might have discovered districts where the thermometer straddles over eighty degrees in the twelve months, and others where the sluggish mercury is seldom called upon to execute a variant of more than a dozen. So also with the rainfall: here it may continue for eight months, whilst two monsoons blow their vapours over the land; and there confine itself to eight weeks of summer showers. To gain an extended idea of what is practicable in the vagaries of the firmament, a study of the meteorological phenomena of England's Eastern Empire will enlarge the mind.

Concerning a conglomeration of countries so diversified in people, topography, and climate, it is difficult to generalise. As we survey the kaleidoscopic whole, the wonder rises to find them under a single rule. One law runs current through all these kingdoms and peoples; one brain directs them. The edict issued at Simla or Calcutta can control with equal force this cosmopolitan land. And yet a hundred and fifty years ago, what is now a prosperous and peaceful Empire was a vast cockpit for warring nations, a seething hotbed of opposing nationalities, and a veritable scene of unceasing tumult and battle.

For nearly fifty years, not a cannon has been fired in anger within the confines proper of British India, and that is the greatest victory the English have achieved in the East. Well might De Tocqueville write: "There has never been anything so wonderful under the sun as the conquest, and, still more, the government, of India by the British."

Let us glance back a hundred years and draw a parallel. In 1802, Napoleon wrung from the English the peace of Amiens—armistice, we may better call it—and compelled them to surrender all that they had won during the war with the French Republic. For the next decade, the progress and prestige of France in Europe resembled that of England in India. Each was a career of conquest. Wellesley, who broke the power of the Sultan of Mysore and the Mahrattas, was, in effect, the Napoleon of India. He carried England into the dominant position. Had Napoleon consolidated and extended his conquests in the West as England did in the East, the whole of Europe to-day would have been under the peaceful dominion of France. Had the English made no better use of their advantages than the Corsican, they would to-day be confined to the Gangetic basin, a moderate territory in Madras, Bombay city, and one or two ports on the Malabar coast. But they had the genius to hold, assimilate, and extend. Where their foot was planted there it stayed, and presently advanced. And although they suffered a Moscow in Afghanistan in the 'forties, they avoided a Waterloo at Delhi in the 'fifties, and rose as high above their difficulties as Napoleon fell below his. India of to-day, with its countless kingdoms, principalities, and peoples, conquered and held by the sword, yet ruled in absolute internal peace, with justice, moderation, and benefit to its inhabitants, shows what a nation can do that can govern as well as conquer.

It is difficult to say what causes have principally operated to bring about this marvellous result; how much should be attributed to the genius of the conquering race for governing, how much to the adaptability of the conquered race for being governed. Taken as a whole, the natives of India, with the exception of a few turbulent Mahomedans, are law-abiding to the point of servility. They are no strangers to submission, and perhaps the English have reaped where others have sown. Provided you do not interfere with their two sacred prejudices,—their caste and women,—they will endure more than most people. For centuries, they have lived in a subject state; subject to ruthless conquerors; subject to pestilence and famine; subject to the exactions of their own rulers. They were pliable material to work upon, and when they came under the British yoke, meek, spiritless, and browbeaten. Instead of oppressing them, England ameliorated their condition, and although their prejudices are monumental, they had the wit to see that their circumstances were improved, and the commonsense to adapt themselves to them. That was in the old days, before they were educated. Notwithstanding they are no older than the 'sixties, from that time began the period of present transition, which is slowly but surely transforming the peoples of India, and changing the East, that has been called Unchanging.

Modern India dates from the opening of the Suez Canal, and the influx of prosperity and civilisation that followed it. Ferdinand de Lesseps did more for the Indian Empire in one decade than England did in all the previous ones. In these days, when one has only to go to Ludgate Circus to take a ticket for Central Africa, it is difficult to believe that a generation ago there were great tracts in the Indian Empire where you habitually travelled on men's shoulders to reach your destination. I do not mean to imply that you have not to do so still—I have a vivid recollection, not so many months ago, of a twelve hours' journey in a "dhoolie" or palanquin—but twenty-five thousand miles of railway have been built since 1870. The railway is the greatest revolutionist of modern times, and especially in a country like India, where the inhabitants are bound in the iron chains of caste, and where nations are divided from nations, and sections from sections, by gaps there were no means of bridging until the third-class railway carriage came, not only to transport them, but to shuffle them up, teach them to mingle with one another, and cast them cheek by jowl in the same compartment. The introduction of transit was followed by travel, the best form of education. People who see a little want to see more; who learn a little want to learn more. The peasant who stole a peep at the train gliding by, his superstitious mind convinced it was a fearful and unclean thing, found familiarity breed content instead of contempt, for it presently developed into a desire to ride therein. Thereafter, he became an unconscious emissary of civilisation, who was never weary of detailing his experiences, and the incentive for others to follow in his bold footsteps. The railways of India are probably the most crowded with passenger traffic of any in the world, and not one man in a hundred thousand of those who use them to-day would have met, travelled, and rubbed shoulders forty years ago. The same may of course be said of any country or continent; but, as we shall presently see, the act of "rubbing shoulders" implies far more in India than in any other part of the world.

I have endeavoured to show by a rapid survey the varying peoples which the Empire contains, but the point is one which will bear a little more detailed treatment, especially as the scope of this book does not admit of enlargement on it hereafter. The main division of the inhabitants is based on religion. They are divided into Hindus, and Mahomedans, the former numbering (roughly speaking) a hundred and eighty millions, and the latter sixty. The cleavage of ideas, morals, manners, and characteristics between them is as absolute as between either of them and Europeans, or between Turks and Christians in South-Eastern Europe.

The Mahomedans are the descendants of the Moslem invaders who, for a thousand years, poured into India from the West, and established kingdoms and dynasties of their own, which found a zenith in the Mogul Empire. Its fall left the country dotted with Mahomedan principalities usurped by the Viceroys who had broken free from the Imperial authority. Inheritors of such a history, it is only natural that the Mahomedans should retain the instincts of a conquering class, and any turbulence or unrest generally arises in communities of that faith.

The downfall of the Mogul was followed by a convulsion of war and conquest, the beginning of which marked the establishment of British power in India, and the end saw two thirds of it under England's direct rule, and the remainder tributary to her. In that portion, she has kept her hands off the only considerable Mahomedan states —those of Hyderabad and Bhawalpur, and the Mahomedan territory of Cashmere, ruled by a Hindu dynasty. The Hindu states include Mysore, Travancore, and those governed by Mahratta, Rajpoot, and Sikh rulers.

The British territory is divided into six large provinces—Bengal, Bombay, Madras, the North-West Provinces and Oudh, the Punjab, and Burmah—and eight smaller ones, administered by Governors, Lieutenant-Governors, Chief-Commissioners and Agents to the Governor-General, the whole under the Viceroy, who represents the King-Emperor, and has been described as His Majesty's Greatest Subject. These provinces include what were once the high and puissant kingdoms of the Subahdar of Bengal, the Nawab of the Carnatic, the Peshwa of the Mahrattas, the Emperor of Delhi (more commonly known as the Great Mogul), the King of Oudh, the Maharajah of the Punjab, the King of Burmah, and the Ameers of Sind. All these were in their day potentates of the first magnitude in the estimation of their contemporaries; many of them the English sued for favours. These dynasties have been irrevocably destroyed by British conquest and annexation—wiped out of existence as completely as Poland.

Besides these two leading religious denominations into which India has been broadly divided, there are several other smaller ones to be taken into consideration. Some of them are very interesting and curious. The wild aboriginal tribes, who declined conversion to Hinduism when the great Aryan invasion swept over the country, number about ten millions. Buddhism is professed by another ten millions, chiefly resident in Burmah, whilst a third ten millions in the Punjab follow the Sikh faith. The Sikhs are a sect apart, and sprang into existence in quite recent times, comparatively speaking. The purity of their tenets, their tolerance, and the cleanliness of their lives contrast favourably with the Hindus and Mahomedans from whom they sprang. Like the latter, they admit proselytes to their religion, but no one who is not born one can become a Hindu. The Jains, numbering about two millions, represent the survival of Buddhism in Western India, and are a peculiar people who may be likened to Quakers. Their religion directs them to do no harm to any living thing, and to desire nothing inordinately. As a class they have prospered amazingly, and many of the wealthiest bankers in India belong to this persuasion. The Parsis loom large in the British eye, and Bethnal Green has selected one to represent it at St. Stephen's. They are an alien folk who emigrated from Persia into

Western India, and only number about a hundred thousand. Their position in the country is purely commercial, but they have the genius of the Jews and the shrewdness of the Scotch. On the Malabar coast there are two interesting races in the Moplahs, descended from the Arabs trading to those parts in remote times, and a small but exceedingly curious community of Jews, who retain the customs and characteristics of the Chosen People, and their ancient faith, although so long and completely cut off from their co-religionists. They lay claim to be the lost tribes, as also do the Afghans of the north-west frontier, whose Semitic cast of countenance is very marked. In the extreme south of India, St. Francis Xavier's converts teem in thousands, still professing the Roman Catholic faith, and there is a Nestorian community whose conversion is ascribed to St. Thomas the Apostle. As regards the purely heathen forms of worship, the Todas and other wild races still sacrifice to their gods in the jungles, where they dwell shy and secluded. There are two divisions of the Mahomedans, corresponding to the Roman and Anglo-Catholics of Christianity, and exclusive of a fanatical offshoot known as Wahabis. Hinduism is divided into an infinity of sects. And, finally, it may surprise the reader to learn that in this subject-land, where men are reckoned by the million and the hundred million, there are less than a hundred and fifty thousand English, and about the same number of

Eurasians, or half-castes, of whom a proportion are descended from Portuguese.

It will thus be seen that religion divides this complex country almost as much as race and language. Intermarriage between the different peoples and religions is absolutely unknown, and with the fall of the Mogul Empire proselytism ceased to exist, and the only persons systematically seeking to convert others to their creed are the Christian missionaries.

Social exclusiveness is the universal rule in India, and in a country filled with varying elements there is no commingling of them. The Indian peoples are organically antagonistic to amalgamation in any shape or form, and hold themselves as distinct from one another in their social and domestic relations as do the different species of animals. It is due to this that they have managed to preserve intact their respective individualities through so many centuries, and hence it happens that the country generalised as "India" is really a congeries of separate nations, and "Our Neighbour the Indian" the cosmopolitan personage he has been described.

CHAPTER II

CASTE

THE Englishman has sometimes been accused of insularity. If so be it is true, you would have to take your definition from archipelago to obtain a term for the corresponding quality in the Hindu of India. For the system of caste has cut him up into a thousand little bits of exclusiveness, each instinct with insularity reduced *ad absurdum.*

Caste is a great social organisation which governs and directs the Hindu in every aspect and action of his daily life. He is born with it; he cannot change it; and he has oftentimes sacrificed his life rather than "break" it. It is the very breath of his nostrils. To preserve his caste is the be-all and the end-all of his career in this world; to break it is worse than the commission of any criminal offence. He will perjure himself and steal cheerfully, he will maim and murder without compunction, but the most abandoned villain will respect the laws of his caste, and yield blind obedience to its rules.

Notwithstanding that it is unreasonable and unreasoning, unjust, arbitrary, and cruel, caste is a great moral force. The average native will lie about everything except his caste; it is a restraining influence on his life, and has introduced a code of conduct (however misguided) into a character whose moral conceptions would otherwise permit it to run riot. There are those who declaim against caste, and would sweep it away—notably the missionary; there are "advanced natives" who declare that it is the real obstacle to progress in India, and has brought civilisation to a standstill; but, as one of them naïvely admits, "the majority of those who denounce it are men whom it has virtually repudiated." In practice you have only to see the result of deprivation of caste in an individual to realise how great is his moral fall when the Hindu is "outcasted." He is like an officer who has been cashiered, or a priest unfrocked; a "rank bad 'un" who has lost all sense of self-respect, however superficial it might have been.

There are four fundamental divisions of caste—the priestly or Brahmin, the warrior, the trading, and the labouring—and these, again, are divided into sub-sections numbering some thousands. Caste is a purely Hindu institution; there is no "caste" in the sense in which we are examining it amongst the Mahomedans, Buddhists, Sikhs, and other non-Hindu races, and even amongst the Hindus themselves, there is a substratum below the labouring caste which has none at all, and is termed Pariah, or outcaste.

The Brahmin, or priest, is a gilt-edged individual, who neither toils nor spins. There are twenty millions of Brahmins who represent hereditary holiness, and to flatter, feast, and fee whom is the bounden duty of all good Hindus of inferior birth. Manu, the lawgiver of Hinduism, who flourished five hundred years before Christ, assigned to the Brahmins the "duty" of "receiving gifts," and declared them by right of birth the lords of creation, through whose benevolence the rest of the community enjoyed what they were permitted to possess. The Brahmins have lived up to the privileges conferred on them, with an undeviating exactitude during the last twenty-four centuries, and their influence is still enormous. They are the brain-power as well as the bloodsuckers of Hinduism; the Jesuits of the East. They bless, curse, absolve, expound, teach, predict, decide, and govern. Ceremonial purification is their monopoly, a most valuable one in the caste system. They are the "Zadkiel's Almanack," "Ready Reckoner," "Everyman's own Lawyer," "Enquire Within for Everything," and *Encyclopædia Britannica*, in the social and domestic life of the Hindu. When in doubt, the Hindu pays a Brahmin.

The warrior's caste has fallen on evil days since the Arms Act deprived him of his sword, and the *Pax Britannica* of the opportunity to use it. His occupation is gone, for only a fraction of him can find employment in the native armies. But he swirls his bamboo staff, so to speak, tells how his ancestors fought in the good old days of foray and rapine, and retains a fierce way of twirling his moustachios. For the rest he has degenerated into an agriculturist, who ekes out a living from the soil. It is a sad come-down for a man who was a famous swashbuckler and fire-eater in his day.

On the other hand, the trading caste has thriven under the dominion of a nation of shopkeepers. Time was when, like the Jews in England, they knew what it was to have sound teeth extracted. They keep their teeth in their heads now, and begin to show them. Especially the money-lenders, who are a distinct power in the land; for much of it is mortgaged to them, and they are rack-renters, more hated than absentee landlords in Ireland. It has often been shrewdly said that if there were another rebellion in India the first thing to be consigned to the flames would be the books and archives of the usurers.

As for the labourer he is what he ever was, a mechanical, patient, ambitionless toiler, whom nor conquests nor social revolutions can put out of gear. He bows his head and bends his back and struggles along in the old groove, using the same primitive tools as his ancestors and employing the same crude methods. The crusted conservatism of this caste is second only to that of the Brahmins. The pride of the priest finds its counterpoise in the humility of the proletariat, and between them they demonstrate the maximum degrees of dignity and degradation.

The Pariah you can hardly include in Hinduism, though he has his degrees. He dwindles off into the scavenger, who is merely a sanitary machine, performing the functions of a drainpipe. And yet, absurd though it may appear, the Pariah pretends to have a caste of his own, and is quite pedantic in keeping it, and cases are not uncommon where, outcaste himself, he proceeds to "outcaste" his erring brother! The species thus arrived at is something lower than the missing-link.

All these castes are hereditary. A priest's son is a priest; a soldier's a soldier; a carpenter's a carpenter; a scavenger's a scavenger. There is no question of "What shall we do with our boys?" in Hinduism; that problem has been solved in advance for two thousand years. For a sire to start his son in any other calling but his own would be "against his caste," and there all argument ends. For caste is both social and religious, and includes the calling as well as the creed.

The requirements and restrictions of caste are innumerable. Many of them are arbitrary, inconsistent, and even contradictory. The principal laws direct that individuals shall marry only those of their own caste, eat with their own caste, and of food cooked by a caste-fellow or a Brahmin; that no superior shall allow one of inferior caste to touch his cooked food, or even enter the room in which it is being cooked; but articles of a dry nature, such as rice, grain, and so forth, are exempt from defilement by touch so long as they remain dry. Water and other liquids are peculiarly susceptible to contamination, but rivers, reservoirs, and ponds are excepted. The higher and "clean" castes are not allowed to touch the lower or outcastes; even the brushing of garments in passing is reckoned defilement, and the shadow of the inferior is considered unclean. There are several prohibited articles of food, such as the flesh of kine, swine, and fowls, the eating or touching of which entails defilement. A person may not cross the ocean or any of the boundaries of India without being outcasted. Marriage with a widow entails similar excommunication, as does immorality in females. The immoral connections of men are not visited with retribution, though theoretically reprobated. Embracing Christianity or Mahomedanism *ipso facto* leads to exclusion from caste.

The punishment of being outcasted may be described as a blend of boycotting and ecclesiastical excommunication. The backslider's friends and relatives refuse to partake of his hospitality or grant him theirs; they will not eat, drink, or smoke with him, which are far more significant acts than as comprehended in our social philosophy. They decline to marry his children, or give him theirs in marriage, and if he have a married daughter she is debarred from visiting him. Those important functionaries, the priest, barber, and washerman, refuse to serve him. All connection with him is completely severed, and no one will assist him even at the funeral of a member of his family, which, in a land where there are no undertakers and no hearses even for the richest, lands him in a parlous predicament. It is absolute social ostracism.

Reinstatement in caste is possible in most cases after going through a ceremony of purification, which consists in swallowing a mixture compounded of the products and excrements of the cow, feasting an assemblage of caste-brethren, and feeing the Brahmins. The latter, you may be sure, are always to the fore, and their services are constantly required for ceremonial purification to atone for slight lapses or accidental slips, each and every one of which needs its expiatory procedure. The cow is a most sacred animal,—it can purge from sin and lead the way to a better world. When a Hindu is dying, he is always lifted from his bed and laid on mother earth, and in many places, the tail of a cow is guided into his faltering grasp that it may pull him to heaven. There was an old cow on my plantation in India that had performed this serviceable function for a hundred moribund coolies!

I have called caste inconsistent and contradictory, and here are a few illustrations. A caste which is accounted "clean" in one part of India may be held contrariwise in another, as for instance, the potters; the Brahmins and Rajpoots of

Northern India eat the flesh of the wild pig without sustaining any pollution, though such an act would render them liable to the severest damnatory penalties in Bengal. The eye is winked at a rich Hindu who keeps a Mahomedan mistress, which would undoubtedly fix him with utter condemnation did he marry a widow of his own caste. A man may sit on his fence and see the land ploughed, and urge the ploughman to goad the team, as he often does, and yet may not plough himself, because that entails driving the bullocks, which are sacred animals. A Brahmin may eat sweetmeats or wheat with men of the warrior or trading castes, but not rice, for that is supposed to admit equality. He may blackmail a man of the labouring caste for food to take home with him to cook, but must on no account eat it in that individual's house. The "clean castes" habitually wear shoes made out of the skins of cattle, yet would be defiled by the mere touch of the hide, or of the tanner, or the shoemaker who made the shoes. The "bearer" or valet who waits upon an English master is often of the highest caste; he may make the bed, prepare the bath, and attend to all the personal wants of his Sahib, but not bring him his food. The Hindu who tends your cows and sheep would revolt at the suggestion of grooming your horse or giving your champion-bred English fox-terrier a bath. The former duty is the function of a low-caste man, whilst only the scavengers may deal with dogs, which are held to be but one degree less defiling than swine. *Per contra*, the cat is sacred, and the monkey holy. I suppose there is no filthier coin in the whole wide world than the India copper anna. It is often greasy with the foulest dirt and grimy with bits of sticky tobacco, into whose composition treacle enters more largely than rum and molasses into naval plugs. But it is cleaner than the low-caste man who tenders it, notwithstanding he may be a washerman, and engaged in his avocation! His touch defiles the Brahmin, but the copper does not. Where other nations purify buildings with a coat of limewash, the Hindu plasters them with cow-dung, which is the universal disinfectant of this people who may not sit down to a meal without a preliminary bath.

But the exclusiveness of caste extends much further than this. In the ordinary transactions of life, when money passes between a low-caste and a high-caste man, the coin is thrown on the ground by the one and picked up by the other for fear of defilement; they may not stand on the same carpet or enter the same room. The low-caste man must not cross the threshold of his superior's house or hut; if he wants to attract his attention, or communicate with him, he stands outside and bawls. In some parts of India, the sight of a Brahmin coming down the highway used to be the signal for men of lesser degree to clear off it. There are scores of these unclean castes, who are, however, superior to Pariahs. I may instance shoemakers, tanners, grooms, washermen, publicans, or spirit-sellers and distillers, basket-makers, weavers (in some parts held to be a "clean" caste), gipsies, and several others. No high-caste Hindu is safe in the presence of a stranger until he has asked him, "Who are you?" The answer places them at once in their proper social relation to one another, for, as I have said, caste is the one thing about which a native of India will not lie.

Conceive the shackles this imposes upon intercourse! What would life be if we had to consider of every person we met in the streets, "Is he touchable?" of every man we sat down next to in a restaurant, "Is it lawful to sit at meat with him?" For you must know that this caste prejudice is not merely disinclination or disgust, but an absolute moral law, which makes transgression an admitted abomination. It is as though a draper by accepting an invitation to dinner from a bootmaker laid himself open to expulsion from his chapel, and social ostracism by his brother drapers, whilst, if he fell in love with the bootmaker's lovely daughter and married her, his lot must be eternal exclusion from the draper's paradise. Locate those tradesmen in India, and I assure you that is what would happen. If, under similar conditions, one can conceive a bishop marrying a major-general's daughter, he would infallibly lose his bishopric and be boycotted.

Caste is respected in the jails of India, where

the prisoners of high caste are provided with their own cooks and water-carriers. The Brahmin felon has every respect paid to his prejudices, but —and this is where the rub comes in—when you get to the third-class railway carriage you override even such a tough obstacle as caste. Into it are bundled Brahmin and Pariah; they sit on the same seat; they rub shoulders who might not mingle shadows. "You must drop your caste," says the railway, "if you want to travel at a farthing a mile"; and it is dropped—to be resumed again outside the station.

The Hindu cannot change his caste, though he may be expelled from it; his social status is fixed for ever at his birth, and he can only fall, never rise. Wealth cannot affect it, and this has tended to make the Hindus an ambitionless race. Nor can poverty derogate. There are hosts of Brahmin beggars who, not even in the extremity of starvation, would feed at the same table with some of the greatest princes, who, although they may rule over great territories, are by the standard of caste unclean. As you may find a swineherd dynasty in Europe, so in Hindustan there are ruling chiefs who are no more gentlefolk by birthright than the English would consider publicans and grooms to be. But whereas in the West it is possible for these to emerge from their low degree, in the East they are ever fettered to it by the chain of caste.

I have known only one instance of a Hindu

trying to emancipate himself from caste. It was the case of a Rajah, who was a member of one of those low castes which are held to be unclean in a minor degree. He expended untold wealth in purchasing a beggar girl of high caste, and bribing her relatives and the Brahmins to sanction and perform a marriage ceremony between them. When she had become his wife, literally translated from the hut to the palace, and borne him a son, his courtiers put forward the claim that the son was of the same caste as his mother, and that as the Rajah had a high-caste son and a high-caste wife, he must be a high caste himself. It was a piece of impudent and shallow pleading that imposed on nobody, and created a great scandal, because it was done with the connivance of British officials. "This could never have happened under the rule of our own Rajahs," complained the caste that had been dishonoured; for caste is accounted a brotherhood, and a slur of that sort affected every member of it. Amongst men of the same caste the appellation "brother" is universal. And in this case, the whole caste, which happened to be a small one, was subjected to much taunt and insolence for the backsliding of the few recreants who had been bribed to give their assent to the *mésalliance*. "Brother-in-law of a publican!" was the favourite form of abuse; a publican being an "untouchable" man, and "brother-in-law" capable of a peculiarly offensive and insulting undermeaning. The Rajah still hugs the delusion, fostered by his fawning and sycophantic courtiers, that he has ascended into the higher scale; but outside his palace there is not a man of high caste that would accept a drink of water from his hands.

Caste is as strict and particular in its alliances as Royalty. It admits of no intermarriage, and as, in practice, every Hindu is married, this hard and fast rule bears on the whole population. The obligation to see his children married is a matter which presses harder on the native than anything else. In the first place, it costs a great deal of money, and often keeps the parents impoverished for years. In some of the castes, large sums have to be paid to the bridegroom for his condescension; in other castes, chiefly the lower ones, wives have to be purchased. There are *Kulin* Brahmins who make a livelihood by matrimony, scores of damsels being wedded to them for their sanctity's sake, as unattractive widows were sometimes sealed to Mormon elders. With the consummation of the marriage, the attentions of the husband cease, and the bride resides in her father's house permanently. In the Rajpoot, which is the leading warrior caste, it is necessary for the girls to marry into a grade or section higher than their father's. When you get to the top of this tree you will find thousands of spinsters for whom there are literally no husbands available. To have an unmarried daughter after she has reached the age of puberty is worse than a disgrace, it is a crime in the morality of the Hindus. Where the wives have to be purchased, the price often approximates two or three years' income of the bridegroom's father. India is a land of universal indebtedness, and the greater portion of the liability is incurred in fulfilling the obligation of the customs relating to marriage.

Within the last thirty years, caste has received many rude jars, and is much less strictly observed in the centres which Western civilisation has pierced. Railways, tramways, schools, dispensaries, and similar institutions, which are open to all, have had a great levelling effect. In the metropolitan cities, liberalism has advanced by strides. The water supply of Calcutta brought the Hindu face to face with one of the cardinal articles of his creed, which prohibited him from using any water drawn from a source touched, and hence polluted, by outcastes. The Brahmins were equal to the occasion, and a special dispensation was granted, though the ordinances of caste were manifestly violated. With the spread of education and the establishment of schools, the same question presented itself in a less acute form, and the high castes swallowed their pride and sent their sons to learn in the same schoolroom as their inferiors. Even in the jungles, a subtle change is creeping in. I have observed, in my own experience, in a district situated seventy miles from the nearest railway, a distinct diminution of caste prejudice. Here are three straws of illustration showing which way the wind blows; I remember them because by a coincidence the first scene in each happened on the same day and drew from me some rather impatient observations about caste. It was in the 'seventies, and I was out snipe-shooting, and, having taken off my wet boots, ordered one of my coolies to carry them; he refused point blank, because it was against his caste. A little later, I asked another to hand me a flask of whisky from my tiffin-basket; he called to the groom (a low-caste man) to do so, on the plea that he would break his caste by touching anything so unclean as Glenlivet. On my return home, a third man asked me for some quinine to cure his fever; I mixed him a dose with water, whereat he shook his head and declined anything except the dry powder. In the 'nineties, No. 1, who had blossomed into my bearer, had special charge of my boots. He was a *Mian*, or Rajpoot nobleman by caste, and the other servants used habitually to address him as "My Lord," and touch his feet with their hands before salaaming to him as a mark of extra respect. No. 2 had so far overcome his prejudices that I caught him drinking my whisky. And as for No. 3 and the "dry" medicine theory, all objections to potions had ceased long before that decade, and rum and chloradyne had become a really popular dram!

As instances of the advance of civilisation and the surrender of caste prejudices, I will particularise four other things which have become fairly popular in India, at any rate where the line of rail runs and the inhabitants are not in jungle darkness. They are, soda-water, ice, umbrellas, and kerosene-oil lamps. At the first blush, they may appear absurd illustrations, but more lies behind them than is apparent on the surface. Soda-water has always been regarded as an English drink; its vernacular name is "English water," and that alone would be sufficient to condemn it in the eyes of caste. And yet you may see it hawked about the streets and railway stations and sold in the bazaars. This betokens a revolution in religious sentiment, for the typhoid germs which Western nations believe to lurk in foul water are not so dreaded as the spiritual pollution the pious Hindu conceives he must be subjected to by the use of the purest, ay, of distilled, water, touched by a Christian. In the same way with ice, essentially an English luxury, and utterly foreign to the native of India. There are ice-factories in most of the large towns in the country, and you may often see an Aryan brother sucking away at his farthing's worth quite complacently. It is a luxury that has entered into native life within the last few years, as the tomato and banana have in the West. But whilst such innovations mean nothing to the Anglo-Saxon, except an increase of his blessings, they imply the snapping of another link in the fetters of caste. My bearer aforesaid, who declined the boots, came in after years habitually to pilfer my snow, in which were laid to cool such abominations as tinned brawn made of calves' heads, the very mention of which would have sent him flying to holy Gunga twenty years before. (And I may here parenthetically mention that in the hill district in which I lived, on the slopes of the Himalayas, I was always able to get a load of snow down from the mountains, even in the hottest weather, though the mercury might register 103 degrees in my verandah!)

With regard to umbrellas, thereby hangs another tale. The umbrella was as great a sign of presumed gentility in India as a silk hat and pair of gloves in London. When I first went to India, thirty years ago, a rising native thought twice before committing himself to the responsibilities of carrying an umbrella, and it was the etiquette to furl it in the presence of a superior. I have seen old Anglo-Indians of the pre-Mutiny period almost go into a fit because in passing strange natives on the high-road they were not complimented with the umbrella respectfully lowered. But in those days umbrellas were costly articles: in these they are turned out at a price which enables them to be sold by the million at something under a shilling. The consequence is that a remarkable demand has sprung up for them, and you will see a man, whose sole raiment is a bit of cloth wrapped about his loins, swaggering about under the shade of a *chuttree*. As for putting it down in the presence of a superior, that is a piece of politeness which has quite passed out of vogue. I can only compare the social elevation this implies to, let me say, artisans in England taking to driving in hansom cabs because, by some unexplained process, they plied at penny fares. Even that would hardly meet the case, for whereas, riding in a hansom is not forbidden to the proletariat, the carrying of an umbrella would have been considered a piece of public impertinence twenty years ago on the part of the great majority of natives, who now habitually sport them under the stimulus of Western cheapness of production. The subjection insisted on by caste is chronically flaunted by the display, by the lower orders of India, of what is, really, an insignia of respectability.

Lastly, we come to mineral-oil lamps. In an age when artificial illumination has been brought to a high stage of perfection, we are apt to forget what a civilising agent gas was in the beginning of the nineteenth century, and how it revolutionised social life. India has for countless ages been content with the dim gloom, after nightfall, provided by a cotton wick, burning in an open dish of vegetable oil; a smelling, smoking flame, only one degree better than the tallow candles by the light of which the English, less than a century ago, were accustomed to illuminate their houses. The introduction of the kerosene-oil lamp, with its glass chimney (invariably made in Germany), into the bazaars of the East is the thin end of that wedge which betokens that sunset shall no longer be the practical limit of the working-day, and promises to open extended hours of labour and recreation to the teeming millions of India, to whom, hitherto, night has meant idleness or gossip. But this is rather an innovation of custom than of caste, and of custom I shall deal more particularly in the next chapter.

CHAPTER III

MANNERS AND CUSTOMS

MANY hundreds of volumes have been written descriptive of the idiosyncrasies of the peoples of India, whose civilisation is a compound of unpleasant manners and incomprehensible customs, as judged by Western standards, and presents to the English mind a source of perpetual bewilderment. Open-mouthed wonder is the permanent attitude for many months of the new arrival in that strange country. To attempt any regular and ordered survey of the subject within the limits of a chapter would be like trying to enumerate the streets of London on the back of a visiting card. In default, I propose to jog the kaleidoscope of my recollection and present the result in the hope that chance may flash a more graphic suggestion here and there than I could accomplish by any attempt at a nutshell catalogue of the subject.

India is a country where the climate takes the place of the costumier, and the population goes unclad. This is the first thing that arrests the Western eye, with its suggestion of indescribable indelicacy, where the ordinary dress of a man approximates a pair of bathing-drawers, and the women veil their faces and display their legs.

It is a country where politeness requires the feet to be naked, but the head covered on entering a room, a bare poll being a sign of self-abasement, and his turban as necessary to the native's sense of respect as a pair of breeches to an Englishman. Take a native unawares with his *puggarie* off, and the first thing he does is to adjust it hurriedly. Catch a native woman *en déshabillé*, and she cares for nothing except to veil her face.

It is a country where everybody habitually sits on the ground and eats off the floor, and throws away the food that cannot be eaten at a meal, and often the crockery ware after once using it; where it is forbidden to eat with the shoes on, and customary, in not a few castes, to strip naked for dinner; where three men out of four consider beef-eating worse than cannibalism; and the fourth is morally convinced that a ham-sandwich could send him to hell; where vegetarianism is the rule, and never an egg is used in cooking; where there are a hundred sweetmeat shops to one public-house, and a native restaurant is an absolutely unknown thing; where every one smokes, but the same pipe travels from mouth to mouth; where every one washes, but no one uses soap; where not one man in ten, and not one woman in a hundred and fifty, can read.

A country where boys are husbands before they

have shed their baby teeth, and brides are married in their cradles occasionally; where there are no unmarried girls under fourteen, and many widows of half that age; where there is no courting before marriage, and a husband may not notice his wife in public, nor a wife so much as pronounce her husband's name; where husbands and wives cannot travel in the same railway carriage third-class; where you never see a "lady" in the streets, and to address one would be considered a gross insult.

A country where more men shave their heads than their chins, and widows are compelled to go bald (though in this conjunction we may recall to mind that less than a hundred years ago widowed ladies in England customarily had their heads shaved, and wore wigs in order to supply the deficiency); where wives wear a nose-ring in token of being in a state of subjection to their husbands; where there is sorrow over a daughter's birth, and rejoicing, or at least satisfaction, over a widow's death; where a man may have four legal wives, and, in some castes, a woman four legal husbands, if they are brothers.

A country where venomous snakes kill thousands of human beings annually, and yet are venerated; where the powdered liver of a tiger is a specific to instil courage; where the tails and manes of white horses are painted pink to improve their appearance, and a wall-eyed brute is considered peculiarly beautiful; where most wheeled vehicles are drawn by bullocks, and no other animals used for ploughing; where many people keep goats, and very few poultry, and no one keeps a dog.

A country which has no Sunday observance; no poor-houses, poor-rates, or poor-law; no places of entertainment or national pastimes; no public institutions except temples and mosques; no public opinion; no political privileges; no representation, and no Members of Parliament.

A country where beggars are accounted holy, and "ballet girls" of loose morals held in high esteem; where the priests countenance prostitution, and often live on its proceeds; where incontinence is not held to be a vice in married men, and religion teaches its votaries to hate, despise, and grind down their less fortunate neighbours; where equality in the eyes of the law is unknown, and the killing of some human beings is accounted a far less serious crime than the slaughter of a cow; where women are treated as creatures born for the gratification of man, and "a man's a man for a' that."

This sample is like a handful drawn at chance from a sack of wheat, but each grain is a solid fact, and there are thousands more like them. Wherefore I say that the attitude of the new arrival in making himself acquainted with India is one of open-mouthed wonder, not unfrequently stiffened with a strong dash of disgust.

And now a few words of general description of

the people who adopt these manners and customs. The Hindu first. Patience and thrift are his predominant virtues, instilled into him in the hard school of subjection, long-suffering, and poverty. He is docile to servility, especially when anything is to be gained by it. Except in the lower castes, he is sobriety typified, and, indeed, by far the major part of the population of India is qualified to wear the blue ribbon of temperance. He has industry of a sort that is not very energetic, for he distinctly dislikes physical exertion, and none of his few recreations comprehend bodily exercise. Sleeping, smoking, and eating sweetmeats would enable him to get through an ideal bank holiday. He cannot be commended as a husband, for custom makes him barbarous and discourteous from a Western point of view, but he is an affectionate father. On the other hand, he is narrow-minded, parsimonious, and avaricious; cheats and lies by the light of nature; and the word "money" is assuredly more often on his lips than any other in his vocabulary. He is cunning and contentious in argument, and his intellectual powers, when educated, are capable of considerable development. In this respect he puts the Englishman to shame, and were all posts in the Indian Government thrown open to examination in India, we should probably see the administration filled with Bengali Baboos and Mahratta Brahmins. The gratitude of the Hindu is in inverse ratio to his greed, and his proverbial mildness prevents any manliness. Although he worships a variety of animals, the meaning of cruelty to them is outside his comprehension. The Indian ox, which is sacred in theory, is perhaps the most ill-used and overworked beast of servitude in the world. The Hindu is callous of suffering, to the point of wanting to make you kick him. He will not take life, but he will watch it, unmoved, dying by inches in agony.

The Mahomedan is a far more virile personality than the Hindu. He is free from the cramping influence of caste, but his bigotry makes up for it. He has been termed "devout," but I think he gets his religion by gusts, which often lead to fanaticism. The self-imposed Lenten penances of the Catholic faith fade into triviality compared with the way in which the majority of Mahomedans mortify the flesh during the month of fasting, when not a particle of food, drink, or smoke passes their lips between sunrise and sunset. The Mahomedan is manly and proud on the one hand, and indolent and dissipated on the other. He is a spendthrift when he has money to squander, and in this respect compares with a Hindu as an Irishman with a Scotchman. The descendant of a conquering race, and the inheritor of a great history, he has something of the Spaniard in him, and lives more in the traditions of the past than in the achievements of the present. At times, when he sees his opportunity, he is turbulent and disorderly. His fortunes have fallen low under

British rule, and he is impatient of the fact. The British eye him with suspicion, and they, "Káfirs" in his esteem, keep him down on the same low level as the Hindu unbelievers, whom, in his secret soul, he despises only one degree more than he does them. Here and there, where he takes to trade, the Mahomedan thrives, but he lacks the patience and thrift of the Hindu, and commerce is foreign to his genius. Intellectually he is on a lower scale than the Aryan, but his unbounded self-esteem enables him to carry his head higher, and gain some advantage from his competitor. He is a tyrannical husband, a doting father, and can be socially a very good fellow if he likes, displaying courtesy and frankness of character. But he is a decaying influence in the land, and nothing short of a miracle can restore him to his former pedestal. In the economy of government, he supplies a useful counterbalance to the aspiring Hindu races, who, having once experienced his yoke, are not likely to invite it again. Between Mahomedan and Hindu there lurks an antipathy too deep-rooted ever to be eradicated, and, in their mutual hatred and distrust, we honest men continue to hold by our own with tolerable ease.

The Sikhs are a provincial folk, yet free from provincialism in the sense of being small-minded. Amongst all the native races they stand out as liberal-minded and capital citizens. There is a nobility about their national character which you seek for in vain amongst Mahomedan and Hindu, and as soldiers they are drawn more closely towards their British officers than any other of the fighting races. Their physical development is superb, and they are a sober and industrious folk. Two of their peculiarities may be mentioned; the men never cut their hair, and, when uncoiled, you may see it stretching almost to their knees, and in a country where tobacco smoking is universal, they abjure the habit. There is a quiet and independent dignity about them which seems to place them on a higher level than other brown races; but in their practical treatment of their women they fall behind the high standard of their general creed.

Of the Burmese, it may be reckoned to his especial credit that he allows his women liberty, both in the ordering of their lives and in the selection of their husbands. In the all-important point of the equality of sex, the Buddhist religion is the only one that approaches Christianity in its liberalism. The subjection of woman in Mahomedanism and her degradation in Hinduism reveal the true characters of the races which, in denying the spiritual equality of the weaker sex, display their baser manhood. Of the aboriginal tribes of India, it need only be said that they are true children of the forests, mountains, and deserts, and you find in them some of those virtues, notably truthfulness and candour, in which the higher civilised Hindu is sadly deficient. They are a primitive people, and some of them in the remoter parts decidedly deserve the appellation of "savages."

Passing now from manners and customs in the concrete, and the people to whom they are peculiar, we come to the consideration of "custom" in its abstract sense, and its distinct characteristic as the guide of life in India. "Custom," an advanced Hindu reformer has declared, "is a god whom our race devoutly worship; it is our religion." You may go further, and say it is the religion of all India, where the *lex non scripta* can overrule the *lex scripta*. The British Government, apt to be a little brusque and overbearing in its financial legislation, cries canny and is most considerate of custom. There are customs in India the law dare not touch which would be considered criminal in England. The word is one to conjure and defy with. When, recently it was sought to diminish plague infection by house to house inspection, custom got its back up and the Government was obliged to cave in. In the statute book are laws quite inoperative because they are opposed to custom.

Dustoor hai ("It is the custom")!—The inquiring soul who sets about asking questions in India will save himself much time if he stereotypes that reply in his mind at the start. For it is the one he will have to content himself with in the majority of his investigations.

Custom is the child of caste; in many cases, it is begotten of it, and inherits its narrowing influence on the national character. It is easy to perceive that the general life will run in a groove when the limit of a man's aspirations is determined by the obligation to follow his father's calling, and his ambition to improve his social status is rendered impossible by the accident of his birth. The caste system is a very jealous and obstinate one, and as iron when you attempt to bend it. It will admit no infusion of new blood, and when the same exclusive spirit is imported into the ordinary dealings of life, you arrive at that stagnant conservatism which is called Custom in the East.

Caste is restricted to the Hindus, but custom is universal. In many cases, it has almost constructed itself into caste amongst non-Hindu races. There is a tendency to follow hereditary callings. In parts of the Punjab, the work of expressing oil is practically a monopoly of the Mahomedans; it has almost come to be regarded as their caste, and they are put down in the census-returns as "oil-pressers." To tell you a man is an oil-presser is equivalent to informing you he is a Mahomedan. The same with silk-weavers. There are some forms of employment a Hindu may not follow because it infringes some law of his caste, and these are in consequence undertaken by other races, and custom soon makes them prescriptive. Moreover, there is a certain unavoidable contagion in caste when you live in a country where three fourths of the inhabitants profess it. You do not ask a Mahomedan what his race or profession of faith is, but what is his caste? In the census returns you fill in your own caste as "Christian." It is the custom. You talk of a high-caste Arab horse, a dog with no caste at all, a tea-plant of very decent caste.

Custom in India frequently overrules common-sense in material matters, and imposes an insuperable impediment on improvement. Look at the Indian peasant's plough. The overwhelming majority of the inhabitants of India are dependent on the land, and their crops would be much increased by better methods of cultivation. The plough in use is an implement which merely scratches the surface of the earth; an heirloom from remotest antiquity. A new plough was introduced by an enterprising firm of manufacturers, and lent free for trial broadcast over a province. It admittedly did the work more thoroughly, and was offered at a price within the peasant's means. But it did not "catch on." Why? Simply because the ploughman could not get at his bullocks' tails to twist them. The superior tillage, the increase of crop, could not compensate for the relinquishment of this time-honoured custom. The antediluvian plough still holds the field, and the system of cultivation is the same as it was in the time of Alexander the Great.

There is a story, well enough known in India, of a contractor engaged in a railway excavation, who recognised that the soil could be far more expeditiously removed in wheelbarrows than carried away in baskets on the heads of coolies. So he invested in some, and showed how they were to be trundled, and flattered himself upon having introduced a useful reform. But that sanguine reformer did not know his India. The next time he visited his works, he found his men filling the wheelbarrows with pinches of dust, and carrying them away on their heads.

The paraphernalia of Indian daily life all belongs to the barbarous ages. Observe any article of familiar use and you will find it primitive to a degree that strikes the Western eye as ludicrous. The pen is fashioned out of a reed, native paper a veritable papyrus, such as the ancient Egyptians might have used, the inkpot a piece of absorbent rag or sponge saturated with a liquid more or less black, and sand still takes the place of blotting-paper. The scribe, who may by reason of his superior attainments be accounted in the van of civilisation, is an individual who squats on the ground and writes on his knees even if you offer him a table and chair. Note the cumbersome native saddle for a horse, the heavy solid wheels of a country cart, the cart itself, constructed with a circular floor for things to slide off from, the artisan's clumsy and insufficient tools, the weaver's prehistoric loom, the shape of the domestic utensils, the machinery for drawing water from a well, the style of dress—ay, of women's dress. Novelty or reform never enters into any of these or kindred things. They retain the fashions of

Before Christ in this twentieth century. Attempt to introduce any other and you are rebuffed with the reply, "It is not the custom." For many of these things there is not the excuse of ignorance. The native has the superior model before him, and deliberately rejects it. It is the crass prejudice of a conservatism more crusted than the laws of cricket, and not to be beguiled by any demonstration. "My father used this article, and therefore it is my duty to use it; would you have me set myself up for a wiser man than my revered parent?" is the reply which stifles all attempt at reform.

But stay. There is one notable exception to this rule which I should be guilty of a gross injustice to omit. The Indian tailor has thrown away his needle and taken to the sewing-machine. It comes upon you with something of a shock when, as you chance to pass through a bazaar, you suddenly become aware of the whir of mechanical action, and, lo! there is a grave bearded man, squatting, near by and driving his Singer, which (to add appropriateness to the picture) he has purchased on the hire system. I cannot explain this departure from custom, unless it be that the Hindu *derzie*, like the English cobbler, is a Radical from the force of a calling which lends itself to contemplation.

When you come to abstract custom, you cannot stir the Hindu off his line of rail. This man will not do this, nor that man that, for no earthly reason except that it is against his custom. This is at the bottom of those enormous domestic establishments which enter into the prodigality of Anglo-Indian life. The combined work of the army of servants is capable of achievement by a general servant in England. But when a European attempts to shift things out of their eternal groove, he is at once confronted with that one reply which admits of no argument in the native mind. And I must candidly admit that the plea of *dustoor nahin hai* is often a conscientious objection, although this does not prevent it from becoming a comfortable excuse on occasions.

In social and religious matters, the despotism of custom is perhaps most pronounced. It leads to preposterous and extravagant expenditure on marriage and funeral ceremonies; it entails long and expensive pilgrimages; it established *Suttee*, or the self-immolation of the widow on her husband's funeral pyre; it permitted, nay, even now permits, infanticide; and the sale of female children for immoral purposes and the institution of the Temple prostitute are crimes created by custom and not religion.

The Brahmins are, in the main, the supporters and guardians of custom; they themselves, whose privilege it is to prey upon the people, are bolstered up by it. Their hoary despotism is the oldest and cruelest custom of all.

Truly has it been said that custom is the greatest obstacle to civilisation. It stands in the path like a lion. It dulls the moral sense and cramps material effort. It has left the natives of India without originality, independence, or powers of initiation. India is a country incapable of indigenous reform. Two thousand years ago its social life reached a certain standard of civilisation, and it has stayed there ever since. The limitations imposed by custom have been the cause of this national paralysis.

CHAPTER IV

FROM RYOTS TO RAJAHS

EVERY one knows what a rajah is, but the ryot is not such a widely recognised man. Yet two thirds of the population of the British Empire is composed of ryots, who outnumber the inhabitants of the British Isles by five to one. The ryot is, in short, the Indian peasant, and in the census papers he comes out easily top of the list with a score of over two hundred millions. He is the poorest man who owns allegiance to the King, and his average income is three halfpence a day. Oftentimes it comes to pass that between him and salvation only hovers a shower of rain. For a wage of twopence halfpenny or threepence a day, he will emigrate to distant parts of the Empire; offer him eightpence, and he will go to the West Indies or the islands of the Pacific. He is chronically in debt, and when his creditors sell him up they are lucky if his estate realises ten shillings. Of such is the ryot as a pecuniary asset of the Empire.

He is nominally a civilised man, on whom caste has conferred an elaborate social system, and he has behind him a history from which he has evolved a policy—patience,—and a philosophy—fatalism. *Khoda jâne!* ("God knows!") and "*Khoda ka merzee*" ("It is the will of God") sum up his speculations of the future, and register his resignation to the past. He has nothing more to say. And yet this humble creature produces rajahs—pages of them, as any Indian directory will certify—as penny fares produce railway kings, or the soil of a flower-bed tulips. In fact, the rajahs are the tulips that spring out of this sad clay of humanity. Without the ryot, there would be no Golden East. He is the atom of dust which, mingled with millions of other atoms, gives growth to those gorgeous blossoms that shed their lustre in England, when Jubilee or Coronation calls them to her shores. Those gems and jewels you see decorating the portly exteriors of dusky potentates are paid for with the sweat of the ryot's brow. A large portion of the eighty million pounds of revenue annually extracted from India comes from the pockets of the peasantry.

"The ryot at home" can be drawn with a piece of charcoal on a whitewashed wall. Item, a single-roomed thatched hut, built by himself, without doors, windows, or chimney; item, a floor, plastered with cow-dung, and three or five bricks, set like a robin trap, to serve as fire-place; item, a rough framework of wood with some coir rope strung across it to act as a bed for the master of the house; item, a few earthenware pots to contain water, and ditto dishes to serve up food in; item, something which looks like a patchwork door-mat, but is in reality his bedclothes; item, a cloth for his loins, another for his shoulders, and a third for his head; item, his wife's petticoat, bodice, and *saree* (into which, woman-like, she manages to get a dash of colour and look picturesque). The inventory is complete. We read in the Bible of a man taking up his bed and walking; the ryot can in many cases not only take up his bed, but all his family's belongings, and trot off with them.

His uneventful life is one of dreary monotony and labour, with a week of seven working days. Perhaps three or four times a year, he enjoys a holiday, when some festival of his caste permits the opportunity. If he has saved up fourpence to squander on sweetmeats, he is a jubilant man. But a little of this dissipation has to go a long way, and his eye is always on the sky, looking for that shower of rain. If it does not come, he is bankrupt. Nay, as like as not, the blue firmament may have his death-warrant written on it.

The field he tills is not his own, for in India all land belongs to the ruler of the territory, and rent has to be paid for it; he is assessed from an eighth to half his produce. If he has mortgaged his land, and he nearly always has, it is never less than half.

If he has no land, he must still be taxed. It is naturally rather difficult to levy on a person whose income is tenpence halfpenny a week; but still it must be done in order that the wheels of the chariot of British Empire may roll on. You would think that a man who was too poor to hold land under the conditions described would be too poor to tax. Excise cannot reach him; it would be positively indecent to demand tribute from his dress, although if in his vanity he demands English cotton goods he has to pay duty on them. But the Government of India in its infinite wisdom has discovered a method of bleeding stones. In the economy of nature, man is an animal who cannot avoid eating salt, and that necessary article of diet has been put under contribution, whereby even the beggars of the Empire pay their tribute to Cæsar. The salt-tax is one of the soundest fiscal resources in India.

In the district where I lived there were some mines that yielded black salt, a villainous-looking substance like dark sandstone. I have known natives to travel three days' journey to those mines, to give a day's free labour for quarrying, and go home again three days' march, in order that they might lay in their year's supply at the cheapest rate. It cost them a week's travel, plus a shilling, and most of the shilling went to Government in the shape of salt-tax.

I vow there is no more pathetic figure in the British Empire than the Indian ryot. His masters have ever been unjust to him, and ground and ground him until everything has been expressed, except the marrow of his bones. Even Nature has scant pity on him, for she constantly scourges him with famine, and (as happened three years ago) exterminates a million lives with a dry breath. A sword, like that of Damocles, hangs permanently suspended over the ryot, and every sowing season, he sees the hair that sustains it stretching like a piece of elastic. Perhaps it is a merciful thing for him that he is a fatalist, and that "the will of God" sufficiently explains for him the multitude of his hardships and the inequality of his state.

As in England, so in India, it is a great step up from the agricultural labourer to the artisan class. The latter are a well-to-do folk, and you seldom see them suffering the pinch of poverty, except in the universal cataclysm of a famine. The system of caste has in practice made a trades-union of each calling, and very definite are the rules and conditions under which members work. A strike, in the English sense, does not enter into the policy of the Eastern artisan; but, nevertheless, he has an acute appreciation of the exact amount of work to be rendered for his remuneration, which is regulated by custom, and not individual ability, and you cannot hurry him.

He is often an ingenious fellow, and his æsthetic sense is proved by his ornamental metal work, his exquisite wood-carving, his elegant architecture, and his masterly moulding. Sir George Birdwood has it that he is a born artist. If you let him go to work his own way, he will often surmount difficulties you would not give him the credit of being able to overcome. I can remember a village blacksmith who was employed as an assistant handy-man to an engineer, and eventually stepped into his place, not only driving an engine, but keeping its working parts in repair. I have known a mason whose wage was sixpence a day to build a house from a plan, when he himself could neither read nor write; and a carpenter on four shillings a week to copy most excellently well the design of a piece of English furniture from the illustration in an advertisement.

In many cases, not only is the calling of the artisan hereditary, but his particular appointment. Each village has its blacksmith, carpenter, and potter, who are communal functionaries, and bound by immemorial custom to render certain services, for which they get what is in effect a salary from the village, and each villager has a prescriptive right to have certain things done for him. But amongst these skilled folk you shall look in vain for a plumber, a painter, or a cabinet-maker, as you may for a chemist's, a stationer's, or a bookseller's shop. On the other hand, you will find many more workers in brass, silver, and gold than in similar communities in England —for this reason, that all the native's domestic utensils are made of brass, and most of his savings go to making silver or gold ornaments for his wife. That is his "capital."

The common carrier does a great business in India, though much less now than in the days before railways. In many parts, beasts of burden, chiefly oxen, are the principal means of transport, and the *brinjari's* life is much like that of the gipsy's. You meet him everywhere, with his droves of pack-oxen, carrying grain and merchandise from distant places to feed the great lines of railway. He seems out of date in this age, and yet a hundred years ago his prototype was common enough in England, when the roads there were certainly not to be compared with those in India at the present day.

Of all classes in Indian life there is no one who seems so admirably suited to his setting as the Indian tradesman. In the first place, he lives in an atmosphere of money, be it silver, copper, or cowrie shells, and that appeals to the national character. In the second place, he can be indolently industrious, that is to say, put in a long day's work sitting on his hams.

In a calling where competition largely enters, the Indian tradesman is curiously conservative. He does not go about looking for a good "pitch," or trying to find a neighbourhood where he will have a monopoly of the article he deals in. Custom has ordained that in an Indian bazaar birds of a feather shall flock together, and the different streets become a sort of exclusive market for each commodity. In this place, you will see a row of grain sellers, in that, a congregation of hardware merchants; the butchers are all established cheek by jowl yonder, and the cloth merchants cluster in a quarter of their own. A morning's miscellaneous shopping takes you "round the town." The art of advertising is absolutely unknown, and the shopkeeper's name is more often than not considered unnecessary above his shop. You would think that the communal system, which is so characteristic of the Indian village, had entered into the trade of the country, and that it was conducted on the principles of a trust, with no need to compete.

The shopkeeper sits on the floor of his shop, surrounded by his various goods, and his client addresses him from the street or gutter. He never rises to serve a customer, for everything is within reach of his hand. He may solicit the passer-by to purchase, but if unsuccessfully, his philosophy is much the same as the ryot's—it is the will of God. If, however, any one stops to deal, he will haggle for all time. Providence having sent a customer his way, the personal equation enters, and he must not be allowed to depart without buying.

The shops in a bazaar all seem about the same size. There are no large establishments, and a Corner Grocery or Cash Stores are out of the question, because each man sells his particular wares and nothing else. There are no shop-assistants, and, needless to say, no early closing. Women never meddle with trade, which is solely in the hands of the men. Credit is universally given, and huge interest added. Short weights are common, and the milkman waters his milk to an atrocious degree. Scales are made of wood and string, and before weighment are ostentatiously suspended to demonstrate that they hang evenly, whilst when it comes to the balance, the side of the hand is always on the side of the commodity being weighed, and seldom idle. A native will brag that he "saved" or "made" so much in the process of weighing. Silversmiths require particular attention, or they will mix alloy with sterling metal. The ambition of every trader is to become a money-lender, for usury has an irresistible charm to the native mind.

The moneyed classes in India are either landowners on a large scale or merchants trading in a large way. They form a small percentage of the population in point of numbers. The investment of wealth in India inclines to land, for in a country where the soil theoretically belongs to the ruler, to possess a share carries a certain prestige with it, and the instinct of the Hindu race is agricultural. The Indian system of registration makes land tenure far more safe and simple than in England, with its intricacies of titles and title-deeds. There is, however, a growing tendency to invest moneys in securities, and the Government savings banks are well patronised. In the head centres of commerce, the mercantile classes have been bitten with the mania of speculative investment, and the cotton market of Bombay and the industrial ventures in Calcutta supply plenty of *media* for gambling. When gold was discovered in Southern India some years ago, many companies were formed, and the wild speculation in their shares was quite Western in its intensity. The spirit of gambling is curiously pronounced in a race that is otherwise thrifty by instinct. The *Marwarries*, or native bankers of Calcutta, wager wildly on the rain when the monsoon is about to burst, and, to draw illustration from a trifle, in bargaining between Europeans and shopkeepers, a proposal to toss to fix the price is seldom declined, and sometimes proposed.

"Hoarding" is very commonly adopted by those who have money, and mother earth is probably the principal of all Indian banks. To dig a hole in the floor of his house and bury his money there is still the favourite resource of many a native, and could all the buried treasure in the country be brought to light, it would probably be sufficient to pay off the national debt of the Empire. In my own experience, I have frequently, in the course of business transactions, had money tendered me in bags the shaking of which disclosed a very fair sample of the soil from which the rupees had recently been disinterred; and I have known much wailing and lamentation to follow the sudden death of an individual who had omitted to disclose the spot where his money was hidden from his own heirs.

The homes of the moneyed classes do not, as a rule, display the striking contrast to the homes of the poor to which one is accustomed in England. Drawing and dining rooms there reflect the taste and indicate the care of English wives, but in India, the woman has no voice in these matters, for her apartments are separate and secluded. Then, again, there is no furniture; chairs and tables are unknown in Indian native life, not to mention glazed windows and chimneys. The Indian has no sense of surrounding himself with comfort, in English home phrase. Cover the floor with mats or carpets, and you have finished his house-furnishing. He would feel as awkward in a furnished room as Europeans would to live in one of his bare apartments. The love of display is a guiding principle in the lives of the wealthy, and if they squander money, they would much rather buy an equipage that will attract attention when they are abroad than furnish their homes in a way which only the occasional European visitor could appreciate, and to adapt themselves to which would be positive discomfort. You have but to see a native sitting on a chair to realise this, albeit the offer of one is the most coveted compliment you can pay him. He writhes in it much as an Englishman would do were he compelled to sit for any length of time on the floor.

High, high on the top of the Indian social tree, whose roots draw nourishment from the two hundred millions of ryots, blossoms the rajah. How many there are of him, big, little, and middling, it would be hard to say (for the principle of petty principalities is as indigenous to Hindustan as to Germany), but it may safely be stated as not very far short of a thousand. How petty some of them are who are, nevertheless, entitled to the distinction of "Rajah" can scarce be credited. One I knew would hobnob with my servants, and his revenue from his hereditary kingdom was considerably less than £200 a year. He lived in a most picturesque old castle, inhabited chiefly by snakes, scorpions, and bats, but he spent most of his life in the neighbouring British law court defending actions for debt. I remember entering a walled town in Kattywar and seeing what looked like a loafer drinking gin out of a bottle as he squatted in the gateway. "Who are you?" I asked. "The King of this country," he replied with perfect truth. He boasted an ancestry that was supposed to go back to the sun. And talking of ancestry, in the published life of "Lútfullah," a respectable Mahomedan gentleman, you may see in the beginning a pedigree extended back to Adam in sober pride and credulous satisfaction.

From the riffraff of royalty, to whom I have alluded, it is a far cry to such potentates as the Nizam of Hyderabad, the Guicwar of Baroda, or the Maharajah of Mysore, rulers who govern kingdoms as extensive as the British Isles in whole or in part. Nor must mention be omitted of the Rajah of Udaipúr, whose proud boast is that he never bent the knee to the Great Mogul. His absence through "indisposition" from the Delhi *durbar* ceremony of January, 1903, when the King was proclaimed Emperor of India, was, I make no doubt, due to his disinclination to yield precedence to other rajahs placed above him.

Officially the nice degrees of, what I may call, the superior kings are indicated by the salutes they are entitled to receive. Thus there are some three or four to whom the compliment of twenty-one guns is accorded on State occasions. From this, by diminutions of two guns, the salutes dwindle down to nine. The greatest punishment that can be inflicted on an Indian king is to dock him a couple of guns in his salute. It sends him down a place in his class, and the jealousy amongst these sovereigns transcends description.

Another mode of assessing a rajah is by his income, which is in practice the entire revenue of his state. As the English talk of six-pounders, twelve-ton guns, and eighty-ton guns, so they talk in India of one-lakh, ten-lakh, and thirty-lakh rajahs, a lakh being a hundred thousand rupees. The rajah fixes his own civil list, and expends the balance of his revenue on the expenses of his state, and his life is often one long struggle to keep the major portion to squander on himself.

The Indian courtier has brought the art of fawning and flattering to an acme, and words would be powerless to describe the atmosphere of adulation in which the rajah lives. To see him lost in self-indulgence is the one end and aim of his ministers, in order that they may be left a free hand. Thus every temptation is spread before him, and every snare set that safety permits. When a rajah takes to vicious ways, it may be said that what he does not do to disgrace humanity leaves very little to be done. Happily the power of life and death is not left in his hands by the suzerain power.

There is a school for young rajahs, where they are trained in the way they should go, and afforded an education on good wholesome public-school lines. It has worked wonders, and is turning out a new race of rajahs to take the place of the old, besotted, obese brutes, who have disgraced so many thrones in the East. The new rajah is a very decent fellow—certainly for some time after he has left school. He can ride, shoot, play polo, cricket, tennis, and other games, and comport himself like a man; dance, too, and behave in a drawing-room like a gentleman. If he avoids drink, and rises superior to the almost overpowering temptations of the zenana or the harem, he often becomes a first-rate governing man, especially if he belongs to one of the martial races.

The power for good and evil vested in the hands of a rajah is enormous, even though he have a British official Resident at his court to keep an eye on how he is conducting himself. No Viceroy or Governor can appeal to the people of India like one of their own rulers. The Englishman is an impersonal potentate; no matter what his status, he is "unclean" to the Hindu, a "Káfir" to the Mahomedan. He lacks colour and picturesqueness, even though he be a Lord Curzon, and altogether fails to elicit the same genuine admiration in an Indian *durbar* that an Indian rajah does in an English assembly. On the other hand, the rajah is in accord with his subjects in sentiment, creed, and thought. He appeals to their instincts with his display. They love to see his elephants and gaily caparisoned horsemen, his silks and his jewels, his retainers and *entourage*. His barbaric pleasures delight them; he tosses money to the multitudes in his progress; he feasts them at appropriate seasons; he is a link between the present and the past. What is the coming or going of a sober-coated foreigner to them? What, even, the marriage of a Viceroy? But when a rajah comes into his own, or marries, or has a son born to him, then is the whole kingdom interested, entertained, and made happy in a round of feasting and festivities free to all.

And if he "squeezes" his ryots to get money to build a new palace, or deck with jewels the latest favourite in his zenana, or to entertain a Viceroy, or—newest and most extravagant whim of all!—to make a summer trip to England, well, there is the land; it bears crops. There is the land-tiller; he is patient and long-suffering. He has paid the piper for ages, and never called the tune. He can go on paying! And whilst his liege lord and master is astonishing the richest city in the world with the glitter of his gems, and the magnificence of his establishment, the poorest subject in the world merely turns his eyes to the blue skies and sighs.

CHAPTER V

JACKS IN OFFICE

WE have seen how India is divided by race, language, religion, caste, and wealth, but there is yet another division, which, although it only detaches a fraction from the whole, still demands attention, because it is the governing element. And the members of it afford an admirable illustration of the attitude we understand by the phrase "Jacks in Office."

The possibilities of temporal power are nowhere more thoroughly appreciated and developed than in India. The Indian official, European or native, is the master, not the servant, of the public. It is not too much to say that the native has elevated service under Government into something very like a privileged predatory caste, common to Hindu and Mahomedan. The "Man in Authority," no matter how humble his appointment, draws away from his fellows, and acquires a definite position and power over them from his association with the machinery of Government. The highest ambition of every native is to get into the service of the State, for it assures him the three

P's—pay, pension, and pickings. And the greatest of these is pickings.

All authority in India is despotic. British rule is a despotism pure and simple, tempered with a bland desire to deal justly. The rule of the rajah is personal, with a corner of his eye on the British Resident to see how he takes encroachments on the revenue for the Civil List. Spreading downwards from these summits, the subtle spirit of despotism pervades all branches of the administrations. The lower you penetrate the social scale, and the more inwardly you explore the ignorant masses, so assuredly shall you find the despotism greater and more brutal. For sheer unmitigated tyranny, where he has an object in view to gain, the policeman of India knows no equal; in cunning and rapacity, the *chupprassi*, or guardian of the threshold, is a man who has reduced blackmailing to a fine art.

The administration of India is carried on in practice by something like three thousand Englishmen, who act as heads or assistant heads of departments. All the working parts of the machinery of Government, its subordinate and clerical posts, are filled by natives. An average Indian "district," as each administrative area is called, is a tract of country as extensive as the largest English counties. The English staff administering this territory seldom exceeds more than five or six officials, to carry out whose orders there exist a company of native clerks and a regiment of understrappers. The actual execution of authority filters through their hands. There is no means of ventilating abuse, for there is no public opinion, no public Press (broadly speaking), and no publicity in India. Conceive, then the result when every Jack-man of that subordinate and crafty crew is bent on making, by hook or by crook, some illicit profit over and above the salary assigned for the execution of his official duties.

In England, a civil servant is rightly regarded as a man of fixed income. Be he in a Government Department or the Post-Office, anything, in short, from a Prime Minister to a telegraph-boy, you know that his remuneration is exact and unelastic. But in India, the native employee of Government would be horrified to think that his income was fixed. On the contrary, he regards it merely as a stepping-stone to making money. Where there is litigation, direct taxation, and crime, there is profit to be derived by the shrewd and enterprising man, and the Indian Jack in Office is the person designed by Nature to show how to derive it.

Bribery and corruption are the rule, not the exception, in the East. In every transaction in life, it is held to be not only allowable but sensible to derive some advantage over and above the scheduled amount. He would be a poor fool who did not avail himself of *dustoorie*, or the customary fee. There is not a single native in India who does not pay or receive *dustoorie* in some form or other. It is the unearned increment of the East. It enters into every phase of life, and, according to the form it assumes, may be a perquisite, a commission, a fine, a bribe, or blackmail. In transactions between the subject and those placed in authority over him, it becomes a bribe or blackmail, and Jack in Office is the recipient, and the whole of the rest of the population the fleeced.

Bribery is ingrained in the native character, and a recognised part of the etiquette of their social system. The inferior always approaches a new superior with a gift in his hand—made, not from love, but from policy, and to neglect it is boorish rudeness, as well as a folly. It is a bribe in embryo, meant to smooth the way for an ultimate benefit. Notwithstanding, the native will affect to be vastly affronted if it is declined. It is called a *nuzzer* or *dáli*, which, being interpreted, means a complimentary tribute. Ask why it is proffered, and you will never get any other answer except that "It is the custom." Needless to say, Englishmen are pestered with *dális*—if they are worth pestering. They usually take the form of a tray neatly piled with sweetmeats, flowers, and fruit, apparently a most innocent confection. But, when the investment is fairly safe, a bag of rupees not unfrequently lurks under the pile of sugar-candy. Say, for instance, you are an engineer, with a fat contract to give out, and a reputation for accepting *dális*, you could practically depend on that bag of rupees when you received a complimentary visit from a local contractor. Happily such incidents are exceedingly rare in connection with Englishmen, and the *dáli* contains nothing more guilty than roses, oranges, and lollipops. But with native officials the case is different, and the *dáli* is the recognised vehicle for a bribe.

It is a moot point with the Anglo-Indian whether to accept *dális* of the innocent description or not. Some do; some don't. In the latter case, they "touch and remit" them, which is supposed to salve the feelings of the donors, whose offerings are theoretically accepted, but in practice returned, as the touching of the heels of a monarch with the spurs is supposed to endow him with knightly virtues. Christmastide is the apotheosis or *dális;* then does every native you know desire to present you with one, his eyes glued on the return chance.

If I have dealt at a little length on the *nuzzer* or *dáli* system, it is to illustrate the national character with which Jack in Office has to deal. Here are a people who voluntarily give bribes; who will have you believe politeness demands it; who are willing, nay, anxious, to expend a day's pay in propitiating a stranger who comes to assume authority over them. Saddle that people with an administration considerably more urgent to receive than to give a bribe, and endowed with an absolute faith in its fitness, and you shall see the art of extortion carried to its extreme. Power in the hands of such a class is merely a lever to extract profit from the powerless; and there are no people in the world so powerless, unprotected, and preyed upon as the peasants of the Indian Empire. I have no hesitation in saying that several millions of rupees are paid away every year in India in the shape of *dustoorie*, or the unearned increment of pillagers.

And now let us see how these conditions work out in practice in India. Every schoolboy knows that the sale of justice in the East is a simple and time-honoured institution. Is justice sold under the British raj? Without a doubt it is. I will pass over the higher native officials holding what may be called Englishmen's appointments, with the observation that they are not immaculate. I could recall a recent case where a bribe of some thousands of pounds, specially contracted to be paid in gold bullion, passed between a litigant and a native judge who was the highest judicial authority in the district. And I could quote several others. But in this rank venality is the exception.

When you come to the subordinate judicial staff, the native judges and magistrates, with restricted powers and comparatively small salaries, you may take it as an axiom that, in the slang phrase, they are all "on the make." Prudence alone puts a limit to their harvest. Of course, no one but a fool would take a bribe often; that would be the surest way of killing the goose that laid the golden eggs. In riding a foul race, the jockey's horse must gallop, and to retain a seat on the bench of justice, the judge must dispense justice in general. It is from the percentage of his backslidings that the venal judge acquires his reputation. "He is a very good magistrate," I have often heard it said of a native functionary by natives; "he takes very few bribes." In other cases, a sad shake of the head, and the mournful, "There is no satisfying him!" has been a sufficient commentary.

Notwithstanding this foreknowledge that the dice are probably loaded, the native of India plunges into the lottery of litigation with absolute gusto. It is a speculation that appeals to him, requiring as it does chicanery and lying. For whilst blaming the unjust judge, it must not be forgotten that the unjust witness is almost as great a factor in the prostitution of the law courts, and that perjury is the basis of all evidence in India; the "fourpenny witness," who will for that modest professional fee swear to anything, haunts the precincts of the courts, and will rehearse you a tragedy or concoct you a concatenation so that even cross-examination shall be powerless to shake him. The actual eye-witness rarely gives his testimony without introducing gratuitous and needless fiction. It is an admitted and notorious fact that the bulk of the evidence tendered in the law courts of India is perjured, and yet prosecution for perjury is practically unknown. It is the "custom"; that Augean stable is too foul to attempt to sweep, and British administration shrinks from the task. It may even be logically argued by the judicial Jack in Office that until Government takes steps to punish and put a stop to perjury, the illegitimate profits of justice may just as well pass into his pockets as into those of the professional liar.

Leaving this unsavoury subject, let us pass to the consideration of those Jacks in Office who have to make their illicit gains by operations less simple than selling justice. That, after all, can be done genteelly and with an air of learning, and even defended in a plausible judgment delivered in open court. The Indian policeman proceeds in a different way. His the open palm and the veiled threat. A "case" represents itself to him in two aspects: shall it be pursued for reputation or rupees? If he decides on the former as the most profitable, then this Jack in Office has no hesitation in applying the methods of the mediæval torturer in order to extort a confession from the accused man. If lucre is his object, it degenerates into a matter of blackmail, and most probably the trumping up of false evidence. The visit of a constable to the most honest homestead in India is like the visit of a wolf. When the inspector follows, it is like a tiger to the attack. "Once get the police in——" is an Indian phrase that corresponds to the English "Once get the plumber in——." The Hindu's hut is very far from being his castle. The policeman literally takes up his abode on the premises, lives on the fat of the land, so far as the victim's family can provide it, and never departs without a substantial reason. Those in England who look upon the "Bobby" as their comfortable friend and the protector of their hearths and homes during the wicked night hours, little know what awful shape his Indian prototype can assume, whose presence is far more dreaded than that of a thief. For, after all, the native can defend himself against a thief, but he is powerless to do so against the arch-robber who poses as a policeman.

As with the man in blue, so in his special degree with every low Jack in Office in India. The surveyor who comes round to assess the land for taxation can find a vast diminution in its ratable value, not to mention its superficial area, if the owner is lavish with his *dustoorie;* the watchman who guards a timber reserve is blind to the cutting of a tree if a quarter of its value is slipped into his hand; the goods-clerk on an Indian railway, under the highest pressure of accumulated consignments, what time markets are urgent, will always find an empty truck for the merchandise that is recommended with a coin or two. Every Jack in Office has his price; it is absolutely beyond the genius of the native character to refuse a bribe.

Perhaps the most wonderful Jack of all is the *chupprassi*, who is a creation peculiar to the East, and a sort of janitor at the verandah. He announces your arrival, runs errands, performs petty commissions, and is a blend between an office-boy and a *commissionnaire.* He lives within hail of his master, and is supposed to possess his ear. You would not credit him with transcendent powers, and yet the way that lowly individual can coin money out of his own post passes conception. He is the front-door bell, and there is no seeing the master unless he is rung. "Wait; the *sahib* is busy," is all he says, and you may wait till doomsday if you fail to fee him. The well-to-do native has a distinct disinclination to being made to wait; it is far more derogatory in his eyes than you would suppose, and he willingly pays toll, or, as you may say, tolls the bell. The poor suppliant with a petition seeks advice from the *chupprassi*, asking if the *sahib* is in a good temper to be approached, and this Jack in Office has always a sound opinion to sell. The power and influence accredited to him are extraordinary; he is in and out of his master's room; he knows all his moods and humours; he will unfailingly tell you when is the best moment to make appeal. It may appear preposterous, but such information in a land where despotism rules supreme has a market value, and the *chupprassi* makes the most of it. I have heard of a case of one man on a wage of six shillings a month who contrived to increase it to as many pounds by the exercise of his peculiar talents in imposing on the credulous and exacting toll from the ignorant.

We have seen these Jacks in Office in their smiling moods when the world is going well with them, but there is another side to the picture. Let the seeker-after-something be too poor or too ill-advised to bribe, and you will see a change in the demeanour of the man in authority. He becomes a truculent tyrant, a domineering despot, who reflects all the lightnings of heaven, and borrows the roaring of its thunderbolts. He is devoid of manners and politeness, he rants and he raves, he storms and he swears, and will have you understand that he is a portion of the governing machinery of the land. He is Jekyl, or he is Hyde, according to whether you fee him or not.

For in India, generally speaking, as the inferior is servile so is the superior overbearing. Courtesy from the high to the low is an almost unknown quality; from Jack in Office to those who have dealings with him, and omit to fee him, an unknown one. When once the breath of a little power gets into the native's nostrils, it invariably issues out in the shape of abuse. The abuse of the East is untranslatable, a thing apart. Englishmen relieve themselves in Hindustani when they find their own tongue inoperative. In the native courts of law, I have heard a magistrate address those he was trying, or hearing evidence from, as dogs and swine. As for merely calling a man a liar, that is usually justified by circumstances. This attitude is not unfrequently part and parcel of native official life, and dropped in private behaviour. Blustering and boorishness, impatience and petulance, are the licensed privileges of Jacks in Office. The practice of civility never enters into the economy of the native civil service.

In common with other bullies, the Indian native official is a currish-spirited thing at the bottom, and he loses none of his inherent servility by his translation to the governing sphere. To his superiors, he adopts the behaviour he exacts from those beneath him. Indeed, his humility is invariably exaggerated towards those whose breath can unmake as their breath has made. He is a consummate actor and Machiavellian schemer, who seldom fails to worm himself into favour. Notwithstanding his roguery and backsliding, he is rarely dismissed from office, being far too cunning to run the risk of that. Moreover, he is supported in his hour of need by the clannishness of the predatory tribe he belongs to. There is much of the jackal in Jack in Office, who only fights with his kind when it comes to dividing the spoil. If, however, disaster overtakes him, and he gets the order to "go," in an instant the fierce light of rapine dies out of his eyes, the bulk of his turban is diminished, the ample starched linen robes give way to meagre soiled garments, his arrogance departs, and he passes over to the meek majority whose badge is sufferance. Second only to losing caste is the loss of employment in he service of Government.

There are Jacks in Office outside Government employ, for you may say that every native of India who has it in his power to confer an obligation is one in a minor degree. The favourite of a rich man—and in the East favouritism is an almost universal foible—who has the ear of his master can always put it to profitable account. The Englishman's "bearer," or valet, has numerous opportunities of turning a penny. The cook, who provisions the larder periodically, does not do it for nothing. They all exact their *quid pro quo*, and never a purchase made for you or your household but pays its recognised *dustoorie*, or commission. Half an anna in the rupee is the established scale, which works out three per cent., or double the ordinary rate of brokerage in commercial transactions. In a strange city, if you hire a *gharrie*, which is the Oriental equivalent of a cab, and tell the man to drive to a shop where you can purchase such-and-such a thing, that jehu gets his pickings out of your purchase. As like as not, you will have been previously accosted by a polite personage, anxious to show you the sights of the town, and give you the advantage of his superior experience for nothing. He is a *dálal*, or broker, and the sign that passes from him to the shopkeeper will put an extra ten or even twenty-five per cent. on the shop's price-list. These are all temporary Jacks in Office, who are exploiting your purse for their own benefit. Your groom, when he brings you the bill for shoeing your horse, blandly debits the amount at twenty pence, whereof fourpence goes into his pocket. This *dustoorie* is paid without a murmur by shopkeepers, who know it is the only way to retain custom. Were it refused, they would soon find your patronage transferred, for means would be taken to render what they supplied an abomination by deliberately spoiling it. Even Government accepts the system, and if out in the jungles you hire a score of coolies or half a dozen mules to carry your baggage, there will be an odd half-anna for the hire of each, which is the agent's *dustoorie*.

All India sits, or desires to sit, at the receipt of custom. Financial morality admits it as perfectly legitimate, and King Custom condones it. So long as it is a sort of allowable brokerage for poking your nose into another man's affairs, perhaps no great harm is done. But the system has ploughed the ground for Jack in Office, and prepared it for that cropping with corruption which is one of the ugliest features of the administration of the Indian Empire.

CHAPTER VI

MEN-AT-ARMS AND SOME OTHERS

UNTIL the *Pax Brittanica* turned swords into ploughshares, India was an ideal land for the soldier. In its social system, the fighting castes trod close on the heels of the privileged priestly one, and men-at-arms were as sand on the seashore. For those who were fortunate there were kingdoms to be won, and for all, adventure and pillage. The feudal system which obtained presented countless posts of command, and a bold heart seldom had to wait long for promotion. But in this peaceful generation the soldier's sun has set, and there is only employ for a quarter of a million of men, where a century ago three millions would have been a moderate estimate of the aggregate strength of the standing armies permanently employed.

Except in the military stations, known as "Camps" or "Cantonments," which correspond to English garrison towns, the Indian soldier is as little in evidence in the daily life of town and country as his brother-in-arms in England. His profession, however, continues to hold its high

6

place in popular esteem, and to have a relation in the army creates a feeling of pride. In popular assemblies, the "sepoy" is accorded a place of honour, and is not debarred admission to the seats of the high, and in private life he is an object of respect and admiration, not to say envy. Nor is this to be wondered at, for he is remarkably well paid and treated. In a country where, as a viceroy has stated, the average monthly income of the population is five shillings and fourpence sterling, the soldier draws a comparatively princely pay of nine shillings and fourpence when he enlists (wherewith he has to feed, but not to lodge himself), rising by handsome increments to thirteen shillings and fourpence. When he has accomplished a sufficiently long service he retires on a munificent pension of tuppence ha'penny a day. So you may put it that he is able to live in luxury and die in comfort.

Then, again, he is elevated by the prestige which attaches to military service under the ruling power of an empire ruled by the sword. He is a Jack in Office, but generally unobjectionable. Army discipline and the nature of his calling lift him far above the blood-sucking myrmidons of the civil administration, and, apart from his profession, as when he is at home on furlough or has retired on his pension, it is ever a pleasure to meet him. It happened that for some years I employed a large body of native labourers, amongst them many boys of sixteen to twenty, of whom a few here and there used to enlist. And when they next turned up, and came to make their *salaam*, well-set, smart, soldierly, respectful men, but with the national characteristic of servility eradicated, it was a delight to note the improvement in them. They seemed to have benefited as much under Government military service as their fellows who went into the police and other civil employments had degenerated, and they verified the assertion sometimes made by old martinet drill-sergeants, that there is no school like the army.

The native of India in private life is a slovenly man when he is in the habit of wearing clothes; the very fashion of his costume is a premium on untidiness, and his detestation of physical exertion makes him a sloucher. You may tell a sepoy by his carriage as easily as you can a London policeman by his boots. And when he is in uniform there are few more picturesque soldiers in the Empire, as London has observed and noted. Hodge, translated from the plough to the parade-ground is a difficult subject to etherialise, even when you dress him up in a scarlet coat; but Kareem Bux and Poorun Singh, togged out in khaki "to kill," with smart *puggari*, accoutrements, and arms, seldom fail to do justice to their cloth, especially if they come of one of the superior fighting races, whose physique only needs the drill-sergeant to bring out its admirable points. Even the little Ghoorka, with his bow-legs, squat frame, and Mongolian features, presents a pleasing picture of smartness in uniform.

In England, there are four international groups of fighting-men associated with the four divisions of the United Kingdom and Ireland. In India, as befits its cosmopolitan nature, the martial races are numerous, and merely to catalogue them would fill a page, and leave only bewilderment behind. The Indian soldier always serves with his fellows, whether it be in a regiment composed exclusively of his own caste or race, or in a "mixed" regiment, in which some companies are of one, some of another caste. Racial feeling runs strong, and leads to great emulation, and the older corps, who have a history (the Mutinies terminated the majority of them), are as proud and tenacious of their traditions as the most famous of British and Irish regiments.

In the piping times of peace, the Indian soldier is a singularly peaceful man. Where his caste permits, his womenfolk live in barracks with him, and the cantonment is a small city in its way, with its own bazaar, its numerous "followers," and innumerable wives and children. Very interesting and curious is it to note the way in which these latter learn to drill and fit themselves for their father's profession, which, in this land of inherited occupations, they usually follow; and to see the little chaps, down to veritable toddlers, going through regimental evolutions and manœuvres with the precision of the parade-ground, is an object-lesson in the hereditary tendency.

The British public has a very fair idea of the Indian soldier or trooper from the opportunities of study presented by the representative bodies that have from time to time paraded the streets of London. Looking at their fine stalwart figures, at the mere height, weight, bulk, and girth of some of them, it is difficult to credit the simplicity of their fare and the frugality of their lives in their native land. Most of them are vegetarians, and those big-boned frames and brawny muscles are innocent of any bolstering up with flesh food. Even in a country where meat sells at a penny a pound, the sepoy (putting his caste aside) cannot afford such luxuries as beef, mutton, or goat, except on high days and holidays. Wheat and Indian corn are his staple food. In drinking, he is even more temperate, confining himself to water and milk. It is not our ideal diet for a martial folk; but what shall we say when we come to his idea of a "treat"? Not for him the amber ale of the canteen, or the nut-brown rum associated with splicing the main-brace. Give him a good junket of sweetmeats or treacle! You cannot offer him anything he appreciates or enjoys more.

In short, the man-at-arms of modern India is no longer a blustering, blood-drinking, pillaging freebooter, but a temperate, orderly, well-behaved individual, who sends a great portion of his pay home to his people in his native village, or deposits it in the regimental bank. Notwithstanding, when it comes to the day of battle, you shall find him not a whit less brave than those heroic fighters who faced the English at Laswarrie, Sobraon, and Chillianwallah. Under British officers there are few tasks he will not attempt, and as the Sikhs proved at Saraghari, the Ghoorkas at Dargai, and many of the other races in the brilliant military annals of India, Jack Sepoy is a first-rate fighting-man.

When you come to the soldiery of the native states, there is another tale to tell, with the exception of the Imperial Service troops, lately introduced, who are as fine material as any commander could wish to lead. For the rest, the rajahs' irregulars fully deserve the designation of rag-tag and bob-tail usually applied to them, and in a service where the pay is not only poor, but problematical, and the pension to seek, they are apt to degenerate into Jacks in Office of the predatory sort. But they serve the useful purpose of reminding us what the man-at-arms of India was in the past, and engender a pleasant sense of satisfaction at what he has developed into under British rule.

So much for the administrative and military classes, the Jacks in Office objectionable and unobjectionable, who loom large in the eye, although they only represent a minute fraction of the total population of India. They are men of assured employment and pay, and by reason of it stand out as a privileged class. The Indian Empire, it must be remembered, is an empire of paupers; nine out of ten are agriculturists, and we have seen what are the conditions of the peasant's life. The trading classes can be passed without particular description, whilst we take a glance at some of those callings which are indigenous to the soil, and have an established place in the economy of daily life in India.

And first of all the barber, no insignificant personage in the East, where every man is obliged to shave, and forbidden by his religion to operate on himself. The barber has an official appointment in the Hindu village, with an endowment of land to support its dignity, and a vested right to the shaving of its inhabitants, which can be protected by legal injunction in case of infringement. With the exception of a few races, every native of India shaves his head, and not a few of them their faces. Amongst the Hindus, the business is compulsory, for sin is supposed to adhere to the hairs of the head, and they can undertake no religious ceremony or rite without being divested of their locks. The dead are always shaved prior to cremation, and shaving the face by the survivors is the outward and visible sign of mourning. The Mahomedan, too, shaves his head (leaving a tuft for the Prophet to pull him into heaven by) but never his chin, although he clips his moustache close to his upper lip, thereby often spoiling the effect of a magnificent beard.

The Indian barber attends his customer, not the customer the barber's shop. This carries him into the home-life of the people in a way which is open to no other calling. He enjoys an even greater reputation for gossip than the barber in other countries, and might, indeed, be termed a peripatetic "Daily Male." From the nature of his business, he has become the matrimonial agent of the East, and, with his wife, arranges most of the alliances, being the accredited go-between and matchmaker of Hindustan. He is skilful with the razor, and will cut your nails, clean your ears, and manicure you after his fashion. He travels about with a little bag under his arm, containing his instruments, and the looking-glass, which plays a most important part in his profession. There is no more essential personage in the daily life of the East than the barber, without whose aid the marriage market would languish, and the dead carry with them to the other world as many sins as there are hairs on their heads, for such is the superstition of Hinduism.

Another important individual is the astrologer, who is naturally a Brahmin, and often the family priest. He, too, may be said to be indispensable to the Hindu, for he is supposed to be able to avert all sorts of evil influences in a country which is crushed by superstition; where a child who accidentally kicks its foot against a stone makes a *salaam* to it to propitiate the evil spirit, and the man who ascends a ladder mutters a pious prayer to it not to collapse under his weight. No prudent Hindu does anything material without first consulting the family astrologer. When a child is born, the Brahmin casts its horoscope; when a marriage is arranged, he fixes the auspicious day and hour; when a journey has to be undertaken, he advises the time to start; and he has his say in the initiation or completion of every important business. In marriages especially, he is a despot, and there are extended periods during the year when no Hindu would dream of marrying. In his priestly character, the astrologer blesses houses and wells, consecrates new idols, purifies people who have accidentally slipped from caste, and officiates at weddings and funerals, for all of which he draws his fees. He is a prodigious humbug, who earns a very nice income by charlatanism.

We are accustomed to speak of the "humble" potter, perhaps because he works with mud. But the potter in India is an artist, and there are three and a half millions in the land. As there are men, mustard manufacturers to wit, who make their fortunes out of what is thrown down the sink, so the Indian potter makes much of his livelihood by what is cast on the dust-heap. The poorer class natives of India dine off the rudest earthenware platters, and there is a caste prejudice against using the same dish twice, which creates an immense demand for cooking pots and plates. Water is always stored in pitchers, and we know what happens to the pitcher that goes to the well.

The Indian pitcher is called a *gurrah*, and is circular-shaped, with a small mouth. It contains as much water as you would ordinarily care to lift, and its price is three farthings if you buy a rupee's worth, or a penny for one. Such a thing as a metal water-can was practically unknown in India until within the last decade, when the empty five-gallon kerosene-tin has been adapted to that purpose, much to the prejudice of the potter. However, he has a monopoly of making clay gods and roofing tiles. Sir George Birdwood, in his striking book on the *Industrial Arts of India*, displays an enthusiasm about the potter, "under whose hand the shapeless heap of clay grows into all sorts of faultless forms of archaic fictile art." The potter is a hereditary village officer, and receives certain very comfortable fees. His position is respected, and he enjoys the privilege of beating the drum at merry-makings. He shares with the barber a useful and lucrative place in the community, and there is probably no member of it who is happier in his lot, and less liable to the vicissitudes of fortune.

The mention of the drum recalls to mind the musicians and dancers of the East, who are in great request at all festivities. The dancing-girl will be dealt with in another chapter, for she deserves more than an incidental notice. The musical artist plays upon a variety of instruments, skin, string, and wind, and manages to evoke from these, sounds that convey the maximum of discord to English ears. Performers apparently derive more pleasure from beating a drum than the average British four-year-old in the nursery. Moreover, their music, such as it is, goes on for ever. Having engaged his band of musicians, the Indian employer insists on having his money's worth. The Oriental concert lasts as long as a cricket match. Tomtoming and twangtwanging, varied with constant and inconsequent blasts from a horn, continue from morn to long past midnight. The orchestra sits in a semicircle on the ground with stolid, solemn faces, which periodically break out into terrifying grimaces as they expel a series of notes intended to be song. That the native ear enjoys it, there can be no doubt, but it is equally certain that it enjoys English music played out of tune. One of the most curious importations into India is what is known in England as the "German Band." This has become a recognised institution in the East, and has superseded the native one as being more noisy, I imagine, and more fashionable. The instruments, with the exception of the drums, are all of brass, and there is a decided partiality for those which assume the shapes of antediluvian monsters, and wind about the person. I remember one such band visiting the jungle I resided in during a particularly auspicious marriage month. Its *répertoire* consisted of four or five tunes, which it repeated with a maddening monotony, and all out of tune. A very favourite tune with these wandering minstrels is *For He's a*

Jolly Good Fellow, and another, *Yankee Doodle*, and they are played indiscriminately at marriages and funerals. The social status of the musician is low—which it decidedly deserves to be.

Entertainers in India are always "on tour," for there are no fixed places of amusement. Conjurers, acrobats, monkey men, bear leaders, snake charmers, perambulate the country, picking up a precarious living. They "pitch" where they can, like Punch and Judy men. I do not remember ever to have seen one who could be considered anything but a beggar; but the better class are probably confined to the palaces of the rajahs and the houses of the wealthy. The population is too practical and joyless to waste money on amusement; the native never gives a hearty laugh, indeed, it is a breach of good manners to do so. How shall you expect him to pay for the pleasure of laughing or being amused? He scorns delights; nothing shocks his sense of propriety so much as a ball, and he calls a picnic a "lunatic feed." You may look in vain throughout India for such means of entertainment as a picture-gallery, a music-hall, a promenade-pier, a recreation-ground, a magazine, an illustrated or comic paper, a pleasure-boat, a horse-race, a regatta, or a museum, except where the Englishman has established them. These things are quite outside the genius of the people.

The native Indian doctor is a quack pure and simple, who works much with nostrums, incantations, and charms. When he is called in, it is often as a resident, for he proceeds to take up his abode in the patient's house, and lives there as long as he decently can. He has no diploma or qualification, and any one is at liberty to practise the healing art if he can get patients. His reputation is made by word of mouth, and did you analyse the result of his practice, you would probably find he was a wholesale manslaughterer. In India, no death-certificate is required, and the coroner is unknown. It is no exaggeration to say that hundreds of thousands die annually from preventable causes. Cremation follows death in twelve hours at the utmost, often in three or four, and inquests are impracticable. Speedy disposal of the dead is not only a climatic necessity but a religious duty. No one may eat whilst a corpse is in the house. Nay, this rule is extended in some cases, and in my plantation, no one might eat whilst a corpse remained within the boundaries of it, and, when one of my coolies died, it meant the entire establishment fasting until he was carried out to be burnt. Under such conditions, investigation into the cause of death is impossible, and when you add to them the privacy of the zenana system for women, you arrive at a premium on secret assassination. That this is largely practised in India, there can be no doubt.

But the native doctor assassinates openly, and his instrument is ignorance. He divides all maladies into "hot" ones and "cold" ones. Bleeding is as favourite a remedy with him as it was in England a hundred years ago. Every native of India, well or ill, is periodically bled, and would conceive himself in mortal danger if he omitted it. A common domestic cure for a headache is a plaster of cow-dung smeared over the forehead. There are many useful drugs in the Indian pharmacopœia, but quantity rather than quality seems to appeal to the native mind. I have often been informed with pride that the mixture prescribed by a certain *baid* or *hakim* contained ten, fifteen, or twenty ingredients, as though efficacy lay in numbers. In this connection, I may notice one thing, namely the quick and beneficial effect medicine has on the vegetarian constitution, which seems to respond to treatment much more easily than that of the flesh-eating European. I have been astounded sometimes at the "cures" effected by a dose of chloradyne and a mustard plaster, which seemed to "touch the spot" with miraculous precision. In my plantation, I dosed many hundreds of coolies for many years with not more than half a dozen drugs, and though I have just previously referred to defunct labourers, I have few sad memories in that connection, whilst, on the other hand, I have many very satisfactory recollections of men restored to health who appeared far more ill than I should like to be.

Perhaps the most important personage in India, if you bear in mind the influence he wields, is the village headman. The village system is communal, and the *lumberdar* or *patêl* is the hereditary functionary who governs it. He is the link between the villagers and the Government, and collects the taxes, on which he draws a *dustoorie* of five per cent. He has many privileges, as one in authority, and makes the most of them; but if he squeezes where he can, he is, on the whole, very loyal to his flock. He is much more than a tax-collector or a mayor, being invested with a patriarchal prestige, and, if he is a man of force of character, exerts great personal influence. In the first place, he is the recognised mouthpiece of the community he governs; then he is called in to settle disputes, expected to entertain strangers, and the effective working of the village machinery depends upon him. His charity is frequently encroached upon to relieve the needy. For another of the anomalies of India is that, although it is the poorest country in the British Empire, and boasts a civilisation two thousand years old, there is absolutely no provision for the poor throughout the length and breadth of the land. The charitable instinct of the people is the only thing that stands between its poor, its aged, its infirm, and death by starvation. Only when a famine scourges the land does Government grant any "relief," and in this Empire of paupers there is not such a thing as a poorhouse!

Whereby begging has become a recognised institution and sometimes a lucrative profession in India. The poor and needy we may pass over with the remark that they are desperately poor and pathetically needy. The crippled and deformed require notice. Such loathsome and terrible sights as you may see are too horrible to attempt to describe. Perhaps the worst of all are the lepers, who infest the highways, and when they fail in obtaining compassion have a power of compulsion in cursing; for a "leper's curse" is a calamity few will dare to encounter, and the leper vituperates roundly when he conceives he has a cause.

Apart from those miserable creatures who owe their deformities or diseases to Providence, there is a large class who maim and deform themselves in the name of religion, and trade upon their deformities. You see them in thousands at the places of pilgrimage, with shrivelled limbs, withered from deliberate disuse, and other incredibly dreadful contortions, contractions, and deformities. These are not impostors, but men who have wittingly maimed themselves and thereby incurred a certain character for sanctity. The tortures they must have endured before the limb dried up from disuse, or the finger-nail grew through the palm, or the uplifted arm was stiffened in its posture above the head, appeal vividly to the charitable eye, and represent their stock-in-trade as professional beggars. Kings amongst them are the fakirs, and other religious mendicants, who clothe their nakedness in ashes, roam the land in thousands, and batten on the superstition of the people. These have no self-inflicted deformity to parade; inherent holiness is their cue, and their craft a complete knowledge of the weakness of womankind. Impudent, lazy, good-for-nothing rogues, many of them grow fat, and do far worse things in the course of their abominable careers, practising their arts and seductions, and under the specious guise of asceticism living the lives of debauchees and blackmailers.

India is a strange country of contrasts; and one of the strangest of them is the stark poverty of the starving, industrious peasant, and the sleek impudence of the lazy, improvident beggar, who masquerades as a holy man and lives comfortably on the charity of the neediest nation in the world.

CHAPTER VII

LADIES LAST

"LADIES first," we say in the West; in the East it is "Ladies last." That sums up succinctly the difference in the domestic ideas of the two civilisations.

There are one hundred and forty millions of women in India, and their sphere is the backyard. This is literally correct of about ten millions, and metaphorically so of the rest. They are not even accorded a back seat in society, for in the presence of men they are not permitted to be seated. The whole duty of woman is to worship and wait upon her husband (who is her lord and master in its most exacting sense), and to bear him sons. In some classes, she had better be barren than bear only daughters. And if she is a high-caste Hindu, the very wisest thing she can do is to die when her husband does, for after that she becomes a cursed superfluity in the community. This again is literal.

Five sixths of the upper ten millions of Indian women live secluded in *hareem* or *zenana;* the terms are synonymous for the "women's quarters," but the former is only applied to Mahomedan households. No male, except the woman's husband, father-in-law, and brothers-in-law, ever passes the threshold of this privacy, therefore no European, except a woman, can write about it, except from second-hand. An Englishman may spend twenty years in India and not see the faces of twenty *zenana* women, and then only by accident. The most he will be able to observe is their be-ringed toes in transit, as when they are smuggled, with prodigious caution, out of a litter into a railway-carriage, veiled almost to suffocation, or with curtains held up round about them like little perambulating bathing-tents. In some Mahomedan cities, streets have been cleared for the passage of dames of high degree, and there are authentic cases of high-class Mahomedans having killed their wives because their faces were accidentally exposed to a fellow-man. Some Bluebeard Hindus have done as much to theirs by way of precaution.

There are races that do not seclude their womenfolk, and castes who allow theirs more or less freedom; the masses have a great deal too much work for their wives to do to permit them the luxury of seclusion. But whether free or confined in *hareem* or *zenana*, it is always "ladies last."

The custom of secluding women is of Mahomedan origin, and its adoption was forced on the Hindus after the conquest of India by the followers of the Prophet, who were sad rakes. The system is now firmly rooted amongst the higher castes, and some, in particular, are insanely jealous about the privacy of their wives. There is no chivalry in India, and a dastard want of confidence in the chastity of his womankind is the most contemptible national trait of the average native. Every right-minded Englishman would itch to kick the Hindu or Mahomedan who put into language his views about the weaker sex.

The inferiority and infirmity of woman is a part of the Mahomedan's creed. He has no respect for her, and the heaven he hopes to win is peopled with mythical *houris*, who are young and beautiful damsels. The white-bearded patriarch looks forward to meeting these, not the wife who may have been his faithful partner for a lifetime. The indulgence of an unbounded sensuality is the Mahomedan's highest reward in a future state. In his present existence, self-gratification is tempered by circumstances. The Koran allows him four wives at a time, and divorce at pleasure. But the economics of population and the expense of matrimony make general polygamy impracticable, and only about five per cent. of the Mahomedans of India have more than one wife. But whether one or four, she or they are mere chattels and instruments of their husband's pleasure. In his treatment and assessment of the sex, you may measure the standard of his moral conceptions.

The sexual status of the Hindu woman is even worse than that of her Mahomedan sister. The

Institutes of Manu, the great lawgiver of Hinduism, define her position very clearly. The wife is the marital property of the husband, and is classified with cows, mares, she-camels, buffalo cows, she-goats, and ewes. She is not accounted worthy of separate holy rites, fasts, or ceremonies in a religion which is compounded of them. All she has to do is literally to worship her husband, who is repeatedly described as a virtuous woman's god. The husband, on the other hand, is enjoined "not to love his wife too much," but only to let her have that degree of affection which is necessary. "The fulness of affection must be reserved for brothers and other similar connections."

It redounds to the credit of the Hindu woman that in the face of these demoralising and degrading limitations she should be affectionate, faithful, chaste, industrious, obedient, patient, forgiving, long-suffering, and cheerful. I cull this list of domestic virtues from the mouths of her own mankind, who praise and imprison her in the same breath. From other sources I gather that, in the upper classes, she is often vain, frivolous, idle, gluttonous, jealous, intriguing, and malicious. These detractions may probably be ascribed as much to the system as to the woman.

The women who are immured in *hareems* and *zenanas* are known as *purdah-nashin*. To be a *purdah*-woman carries a certain distinction with it. It is an inference of wealth and respectability, and a man's social standing in his own class depends a good deal on whether he can afford to keep his womenfolk secluded or not. In some castes, where it is not enforced by custom, there is a tendency to "affect *zenana* seclusion." The women themselves are said to take a pride in it, as the Chinese ladies do in contracted feet, and where, through a reverse of fortune, *zenana* ladies have been compelled to abandon the *purdah* to seek their livelihood, it has been as a parting from respectability. And yet, in our Western view of things, *zenana* life may be likened to imprisonment in the second class. It is confinement of the most rigorous description, coupled with segregation of sex, and deprivation of air, exercise, society, occupation, and scene. But in India, it is certainly genteel, not to say obligatory, for most who adopt it.

And we have a consensus of men's opinion in declaring that these poor captives are not unhappy. Even lady-missionaries have admitted as much. The stale, stock simile of the caged canary is quoted, and we are told that absolute ignorance of what they lose by confinement prevents any hardship in it. Perhaps it is so; there are worse fates than that of the well-to-do *zenana* wife, as we shall come to see.

Of course we hear of unhappiness in the *zenana*, but it is nearly always attributable to causes other than the misery of physical confinement. At the same time, we are told the life develops and stimulates the worst passions, and gives rise to intrigue, jealousy, envy, and murderous hate. Mrs. Bishop, the well-known traveller, relates how she had been asked more than a hundred times by inmates of *zenanas* for drugs to be used for disfiguring rival wives or killing their offspring. Crime is safe and easy in the *zenana*, for even the law halts on the threshold, and where the husband's favour comprehends the entire creed of the wife, polygamy cannot fail to be fruitful of envy, hatred, malice, and all uncharitableness.

Enforced or voluntary idleness, absence of occupation, and want of education are greater factors for evil than deprivation of physical freedom. In the higher ranks of life, the *zenana* lady lives a stagnant existence, and dress and jewels absorb most of her time and attention. It is a curious thing that, although she may never be seen in public, and has no opportunities to display her charms, she takes an engrossing interest in her personal appearance. Rouge, menddhal, collyrium, and other cosmetics are common in a *hareem*, and the examination of garments and ornaments is the first and almost the sole form of entertainment when visiting or receiving women friends.

That life, under such circumstances, becomes demoralising goes without saying. The *zenana* woman is mentally and physically stunted and crippled. From year's end to year's end a small sun-baked court in the day is the only place in which she can obtain any exercise, and in city life her promenade is often confined to the flat roof of the house. No chance of physical development is hers, and the Indian lady is always weakly, and often sickly. Consumption is a common disease. To be required to walk any distance is an actual hardship; when it is possible most ladies are carried in litters, and if compelled to use their own feet have a peculiar shuffling walk that betokens incapacity. Their mental development is equally restricted, and there is no ignorance so profound, no inexperience of the alphabet of practical life so pitiful, as theirs. At the age of thirty, their intellectual attainments are less than those of children. They cannot read, their range of observation is limited to their prison boundaries, and the outer world is absolutely unknown to them. Their conversation is inane and frivolous, and reflects the emptiness of their minds. Their husbands confine their discourse with them to domestic affairs, carefully avoiding every topic that requires the exertion of reason, and the result, in the words of one such husband, is "a supine vacuity of thought."

The *hareem* has often been called a gilded cage; here is a description of one, and the fine lady who inhabited it. It was sumptuously furnished with the richest and costliest rugs and pillows; the divans were draped in different coloured silks to suit the season; the vessels for eating and drinking were of gold and silver, and the bathroom lined with full-length mirrors. The lady was bathed four or five times a day, and used the most expensive soaps and perfumes to preserve her beauty. Her powder boxes were of silver, and those for her eyebrow powder of gold; her toilet table was covered with silver slabs. Her collection of jewels contained every known gem. She spent her time in devising new ornaments, and in rich eating. *Au reste*, she did not know her letters, and was utterly incapable of attending to her commonest wants.

This, of course, was a *grande dame*. In the less favoured ranks, the apartments are more often than not squalid, the walls and floors merely smeared with cow-dung plaster, and dirt and the olfactory evidence of bad sanitation everywhere present. The courtyard, into which the rooms open out, is filled with the sheds wherein the cattle are kept, and the "cage" is a dark, drear, unwholesome place to pass a lifetime in. There are *zenana* wives who have never left their husbands' houses from the time they entered them as brides, until they were grandmothers. Conceive what that means—a life without a walk in the open air! Where the system is obligatory and the husband poor, the *zenana* is a prison too terrible to contemplate.

When you get to those classes which permit their womenfolk freedom, the physical improvement is at once apparent. The Indian woman who is not confined is renowned for her grace; she is supple, elegant, erect, and, where she is called upon to exercise her physical powers, strong. In the labouring ranks of life her powers of endurance are marvellous. In the rice-growing districts, you may see the peasant women toiling from sunrise to sunset, knee-deep in the noisome slush, weeding their crops. Their primitive standard of civilisation includes many duties assigned to women, such as husking rice, carrying loads, using the hoe, and chopping wood, which entail terribly hard labour. As carriers, they are able to bear extraordinary burdens, and amongst the hill women of the Himalayas are individuals capable of phenomenal feats. I have frequently seen them toiling along under a load of a hundredweight and a half, and there is a record of one Thibetan woman who carried a cottage piano on her back up a steep ascent of three thousand feet, to deliver it at a house in the sanatorium of Darjeeling. In agricultural and kindred pursuits, the women take their share, and often more than their share, of the labour of men. What his wife *can* do, that the native husband will always make her do.

Maternity comes easy to the peasant's wife. I remember the case of a woman starting off, as she believed, the day before her confinement was due, to go to her parents' home. The distance was twenty miles, and she carried her baggage with her, though that does not ordinarily comprehend more than a blanket and a water-vessel. Halfway on the road to her home she was taken with the pangs of labour, gave birth to a child, and then, thinking it not worth while to pursue her journey, returned to where she had started from. She was the wife of one of my grooms, and I can vouch for this story as absolutely correct.

Notwithstanding the comparative freedom they enjoy, the instinct of reserve remains very marked, even in the lowest grades of women. I never remember to have been addressed first by one, though I employed many hundreds on my plantation. On pay days, when they had to come up for their wages, the veriest old harridan would veil her face with her *sari* and take her money quite coyly. Although amazing chatterboxes amongst themselves, they are silent, or at most monosyllabic, in men's company. In meeting men on the road, they instinctively turn their heads from view; but what is a gentle, well-bred timidity in the high-caste woman, assumes a sort of foolish shamefacedness in her humbler sister, the result of conscious sexual inferiority.

A woman may not walk by the side of her husband, but only follow respectfully behind him; she may not eat with him, but must content herself with his leavings after he has finished. If he fasts, the good wife ought to fast too. She must not speak with him in the society of others, nor may he notice her. In mixed company, the man's wife is the last female you would take to be such, if you regarded their mutual relations. She must never presume to pronounce his name; he is always "my lord," or "my master." She has absolutely no part in society; she may not make herself heard; she has no opinion; she may not seat herself in the company of men. It is a gross breach of etiquette to ask a husband how his wife is. "How is your house?" is the limit of courtesy even amongst old friends. Abject submission at home has created in the woman a sense of helplessness and bewilderment abroad. She is as "lost" as a nun might be. The custom which prescribes her conduct towards her husband is far stricter in its regulation of her behaviour towards others of his sex. "Whether a woman be old or young," lays down Manu, the lawgiver, "she must ever be dependent. In her childhood, she must be in subjection to her parents; in her youth, to her husband; and in her old age, to her children." And from highest to lowest, from *purdah-nashin* to peasant wench, this rule of life is inflexibly adhered to. It is ladies last and ladies least in every grade of society.

The patriarchal system obtains in India, and the sons when they marry bring their wives home to the paternal roof, whilst the daughters go forth to live in their husbands' homes. You may often see three or four generations under one roof, and no Indian wife is mistress of her home till all her elders have died off. All Indian girls are married when they are quite children, and are either wives or widows before they are fourteen. Their marriage is a complete dissolution of their home ties, and opens the door to an absolutely new life.

In the higher castes, the father may not visit his daughter's home, especially where he has dowered her. I have heard a man assert with satisfaction that he had not even drunk water from the well of the village in which his daughter had gone to make her home.

A native wedding is a tremendous affair. It often means years of debt and difficulty, for the native is nothing if he is not prodigal on these occasions. All his thrifty qualities go by the board in one hurricane of extravagance, and it is a case of in for a penny, in for a pound, for this is an occasion when no one dare be niggardly. Here, again, the curse of "custom" creeps in, for these lavish displays cannot be defended by any rational argument.

Every one is invited, and there are dinners for all; nay, in some cases, seven dinners all round. The Brahmins have to be fed and fee'd, musicians and dancing-girls hired, fireworks to be exploded, rich gifts to be provided, dowries to be scraped together, trousseaux to be given which shall bear the test of woman's criticism, and litters or horses hired to carry the bride and bridegroom.

This is the one supreme day in the life of an Indian woman. Ever since she could understand, she has been taught to look forward to it. It is associated in her mind with all that is glorious and grand. She is arrayed in the splendour of vivid colours and tinsel; attention is paid to her; for once in her life she is "somebody."

And her marriage vows? Listen to what the sacred Hindu books say: "There is no other god on earth for a woman except her husband. Be he deformed, aged, infirm, diseased, offensive in manners, choleric, debauched, immoral, a drunkard, a gambler, a lunatic, blind, deaf, dumb, or crippled; in a word, let his defects and wickedness be what they may, a wife should lavish on him all her attention." That is the risk every Hindu girl has to accept with a stranger before she is twelve years old. After her wedding, she returns to her father's house until she is physically old enough to go to her husband's.

The Mahomedan girl's life is somewhat better, for she is not married until she is of an age to join her husband. Moreover, she has certain "rights," one of which is the power to divorce her husband. Also, she may marry again. But neither Hindu nor Mahomedan brides have the slightest voice in the selection of their spouses.

In all India, there is only one class of women which emerges from the fetters of ignorance, reserve, and abject submission. This is the nautch-girl, or dancing-girl. She is a professional prostitute and public entertainer. It is necessary to educate her to fit her for her profession and duties, and so it comes to pass that she can read. She is early instructed in this, and also in singing and dancing, and all the accomplishments. She begins to chant lewd songs as soon as she has finished prattling, and for centuries has enjoyed the sole monopoly of education amongst Indian womankind. And—can it be believed?—the nautch-girl has not only a recognised, but an exalted, place in the religious and social life of the Hindus. No discredit attaches to her calling, but, on the contrary, a great deal of *éclat*. She is considered a necessary adjunct in the temple and the home. Her presence at weddings is auspicious, and she it is who fastens the wedding-necklace round the bride's neck, an act which corresponds to the placing of the wedding-ring with us. In her professional capacity, she is invited to all native festivals, and to entertainments given in honour of guests. To patronise her is considered meritorious, and she fills a place in the Hindu religion corresponding to that which the nun holds in Christianity, for she is consecrated to one or other of the impure Hindu deities. A proverbial saying declares that without the jingling of the nautch-girl's anklets a dwelling-place does not become pure!

She is a beautiful abomination who has lured thousands, and will lure thousands more, to ruin. Attractive, pleasing, and witty in conversation, she is the most accomplished of courtesans, and specially educated to play havoc with men's morals and money. She is treated by all castes with the utmost deference, and even allowed to sit in the assemblies of the great by men who would not permit their own wives and daughters a similar honour. She moves more freely in society than public women in civilised countries are allowed to do, and greater attention and respect are shown to her than to married women. In some parts of India, she is treated with the distinction of a princess.

The earnings of these dancing-girls are enormous. In Bombay the "star" nautch-girls command a fee of fifty pounds for a single night's performance. Aristocratic families lavish their wealth on them, and a British viceroy, who was memorialised by the Hindu Social Reform Association to discountenance them on the grounds that they were "professional prostitutes, lowered the tone of society, tended to destroy family life, and brought ruin to property and character" —a British viceroy answered that "he had seen nothing objectionable in the nautches he had witnessed; they were in accordance with the custom of the country, and he declined to take any action." Truly, great is "custom," and it will prevail!

To these educated courtesans, the Hindu gentleman habitually turns when he desires the companionship his own home cannot supply. And, be it noted, without any stigma or suspicion of wrong-doing. The nautch-girls are the only women who move freely in men's society in India; they are the women who are honoured and courted most; for them alone is education decreed. They are the queens of native society. It is a salient commentary on the domestic life of the Indian Empire that the woman who comes last in the British estimate of the sex comes first in theirs.

CHAPTER VIII

WOMAN'S WRONGS

"WOMAN'S Rights" is the unabashed demand of the New Woman in the West; "Woman's Wrongs" is the whispered appeal of the few who dare ventilate the subject in the East, where native social reformers have been outcasted and excommunicated for striving to improve the domestic position of the weaker sex. Those two cries crystallise the contrast between the women of the two worlds. Up to now, we have been contemplating woman's life in India from its best point of view—the virtuous wife not discontented with her lot, the accomplished courtesan queening it in society. Each in her lights and in her sphere is to be reckoned fortunate and happy. We now pass to the consideration of darker pictures.

There are four hideous horrors in the treatment accorded to the female sex in India—child-marriage, enforced widowhood, compulsory prostitution, fostered by religion, and infanticide confined to female infants. In comparison with the three former, the latter may almost be said to be humane.

8

Infanticide is daughter-slaughter, and is chiefly practised by the rajpoots, who have a reputation for chivalry towards women! It is a direct outcome of caste and custom, and an act of callous selfishness. The Hindu religion makes the marriage of a daughter obligatory, and threatens the parents with the most dire punishment if it is postponed after the year of puberty—punishment on a par with other Hindu religious penalties, which ordinarily include disgrace in this life and several million years in hell in the next. In the case of the rajpoot, the social rule requires him to procure as a husband for his daughter a man of a higher clan than his own. This is often difficult, and always expensive. The payment of a large dowry can be avoided only by incurring the stigma of an inferior alliance, against which the abnormal rajpoot pride revolts. He cuts the Gordian knot by the simple process of killing his infant daughter, either by strangling at birth, giving her an opium pill, covering the mother's nipple with poison to be taken in with the first sustenance, or by neglect and starvation. Under native rule the practice was universal; under the British Government it has been greatly reduced, but has not disappeared altogether. A writer in 1818 mentions that amongst the offspring of eight thousand rajpoots in a particular district there were probably not more than thirty females living of the same caste or clan as the men. When the Infanticide Act of 1890 was passed, the worst case quoted, as proving its necessity, was that of a tribe where the proportion of girls to boys alive was eight to eighty. In one district several hundred children were returned as "carried off by wolves," all of whom were girls! The difficulty of the detection, and through it the prevention, of this crime lies in the fact that the murderer undoubtedly possesses the sympathy of his fellow-caste men. The death of a daughter, before the expense of marrying her has to be incurred, is a matter for devout thankfulness and cordial congratulation in many cases.

Thus we see that woman's wrongs in India begin with her birth, when she is sometimes killed, and assuredly never welcomed. The next injustice is the disposal of her person in childhood, which does not always take the form of marrying her to a husband. The Hindu religion requires brides for the idols who represent its deities. They are called *Devidasis*, *Muralis*, and other names, and their duties are to dance at the shrines, sing obscene hymns, and generally delight the gods, and pander to the lusts or avarice of the priests of the temples. They are a recognised religious institution.

These temple girls are obtained when quite young by purchase or gift. In the former case, the parents sell their daughters when they are children ; in the latter, the girl is a thank-offering made by Hindus of certain castes for recovery from illness or relief from misfortune. Occasionally a man presents his own offspring, but if he is rich, it is considered more respectable to buy a poor person's daughter and present her. But in neither case is there any sense of shame attached to the sacrifice, and in the contorted morality of the Hindus, the profession to which the girl is consigned is a most honourable one, and carnal intercourse with the temple girls "an act of faith and worship, and, according to some writers, it effaces all sins"! There are thousands of these poor girl-slaves in the temples of India, who are the common property of the priests, and were consigned to their infamous lives in the name of religion whilst they were yet, what we should call, "in the nursery." If they give birth to daughters, the latter are always brought up in the mother's profession. There is no lack of recruits, who are accepted from all castes. Sometimes there is an initiatory ceremony, when the girl is formally married to a dagger, the wedding being conducted with all the pomp and circumstance that would be observed in her marriage to a husband.

The temple girl is the only Hindu woman who has any place or share in the rites and observances of religion, and in the same way that her professional sister, the nautch-girl, holds a most esteemed place in Hindu society, so the *Devidasi* stands next in importance to the holy priests who sacrifice at the shrine. In some of the temples, the religious establishments are enormous, as for instance at that of Juggernauth at Puree, where about six hundred persons are employed. The idol is treated as if it were a human being; there are officiating priests to perform such offices for it as taking it to bed, awakening it, giving it water, washing its face, offering it a toothbrush, counting its robes, feeding it with rice, carrying its umbrella, and telling it the time. And to delight the idol, but more particularly the priests, there are a hundred and twenty temple girls, who exercise a religious ministry, and are termed brides of the gods.

Perhaps the most inhuman wrong practised on the women of India is child-marriage. As I have mentioned, every Hindu girl is a wife or widow at fourteen, and in many parts of India much younger. Girls have actually been married before they were a year old, and when from four to six years of age, they very commonly cease to be "single." Eight is a marriageable age, and twelve is the maximum, except in a few districts. Consummation of marriage takes place at the earliest possible date nature allows, and it is here that revolting abuse has long established itself.

The surrender of a child-wife to her husband at a totally immature age has been the custom in India for all ages. It is one of those iniquitous institutions with which the British Government has ever been chary of dealing, for it stops short of actual murder. But about ten years ago, the publication of the terrible and tragic details in connection with the death of a child-bride raised such a storm of indignation that it compelled legislation in the name of civilisation, and the "age of consent" was raised to twelve years by enactment. Prior to this, many marriages had been consummated at ten. But to legislate and to carry legislation into effect in the *zenana* are two very different things, and when legislation goes against old-established custom and religion, it often becomes inoperative. Nearly fifty years ago, Lord Canning legalised the remarriage of widows, but the statistics of to-day show that out of approximately twenty-three millions of Hindu widows only about twenty-five are remarried annually! The Hindu considers it wrong to withhold a wife from her husband when she has reached the age of puberty, and no legislation can prevent it when the parents of the bride and the husband's household are in agreement.

Of course, the physical development in a tropical country explains in a measure what would be impossible in our own. Instances are on record of Hindu women being great-grandmothers at forty-eight, each generation having given birth to daughters at the age of twelve. Wives have been sent to their husbands' houses at the age of eight. Nor does the inhumanity of it end here, for although child-wives are more frequently married to child-husbands, there are hundreds of thousands of cases where the husband is a man of forty, fifty, or even sixty, and the child-wife may be his fourth or fifth. The State of Mysore, which in this respect is considerably in advance of the rest of India, passed a law in 1894 prohibiting the marriage of girls under eight years of age, and absolutely forbidding the marriage of men of fifty and upwards with girls under fourteen. A similar Marriage Bill introduced into the Madras Legislative Council was rejected, and the British Government, with its peculiar sensitiveness to interfering with the social customs of the natives, has done nothing.

It would be impossible to exaggerate the evils of child-marriage. Physically, it leads to torture, deformity, constitutional ill-health, and, as has been indicated, even to death by violence. It produces weak and sickly offspring, and nips the sentiment of maternal love. I have heard of a child-mother who was accustomed slyly to pinch her infant to make it cry, so as to induce her elders to take it, and release her to play. Happy for the child-wife if she has the spirit to play! When she goes to her husband's house, it is to an utterly strange place, where, under the patriarchal system of the Hindus, she has to subordinate herself not only to her mother-in-law, but to all the elder generation of women in the house. It is pitiable for the child-wife, torn from a home that contained all she knew of happiness, to be obliged to submit herself to the temper, caprice, and often tyranny of her husband, but when to this is added the despotism and cruelty of several elderly women, who often avail themselves of her helplessness, and if she fails to find favour in her husband's eyes, almost invariably take their cue of unkind conduct from him, her lot may be better imagined than described. She has absolutely no place to go to for comfort and sympathy if it is not to be found in her new home. There is no escape, and no matter what her sufferings, her parents' home is closed to her. An appeal to them meets with a rigid command to submit herself to her husband.

Mrs. Fuller, in her book on the *Wrongs of Indian Womanhood*, gives a very pitiful illustration of an unhappy child-marriage, which may be taken as typical of thousands of others. A young Brahmin lad of sixteen was married to a girl of nine, who went to reside with him a year later. "The girl's appearance did not suit the young husband, and if she went near him to serve him with food, he would hit her on the crown of her head with his knuckles. Though she was but ten, yet they expected her to do every kind of work. She did the household work, brought water for all, cleaned the utensils and floor, did the washing, milked the cow, and kept its stable clean. If the cow did not yield the proper quantity of milk, she was punished. . . . Her father-in-law would hang her up to the beam of the roof and beat her pitilessly. He would sometimes suspend her to the same place by her ankles, and under her head, thus suspended, place a vessel with red-hot coals, on which he sprinkled red pepper to almost suffocate her. Sometimes, when he had hung her to the rope, for fear she should be tempted to break the rope, and fall, he would lay branches of prickly pear on the floor beneath her. Once or twice, this man inflicted on her punishments which decency forbids us to relate. . . . When her father heard of all this cruelty, he exhorted her not to run away, but to stay and die." In those last three words, you may sum up the life sentence that Hinduism passes on the Indian wife. The father would have been disgraced had his daughter left her brutal husband's home, and the woman's wrongs did not count in the balance when his own interests were threatened.

You might think that under such conditions widowhood would become a compensation, instead of which it is the crowning curse of Indian womanhood. For twenty centuries, the custom of suttee or the self-immolation of widows, existed in India, and presents the best commentary on the state of widowhood. Even within the last twenty years, cases have occurred in the native State of Nepaul. It is true that the act of suttee was held to be most meritorious, and supposed to secure the widow three hundred and fifty million years of connubial felicity, and assure salvation to her family for seven generations; but such visionary rewards probably had less influence in inducing widows to face the frightful ordeal than the knowledge of what their future lot would be.

The lot of the Hindu widow has not changed, and, in the words of one of the social reformers of the race, it is described as "Cold Suttee."

Briefly speaking, the Hindu widow is condemned to perpetual mourning, mortification, and degradation. Her first sacrifice is her hair, which is shaved off, the popular belief being that it binds her husband's soul in hell until she parts with it. In which connection, I may mention the case of an old man and his wife who caught the plague; he predeceased her by four hours, and yet, in the interim, although she was senseless and moribund, her head was shaved. To return to the widow's lot. She is compelled to dress in the commonest and coarsest garments, to relinquish all her ornaments and jewels, and to display no emblem and enjoy no privilege of the married state. She may eat only one meal a day and has to fast twice a month. She is precluded from attending any festivity, must never presume to feast or try to enjoy herself, and be careful not to allow her shadow to fall on food or water that is about to be eaten or drunk. She is regarded as carrying ill-luck with her wherever she goes, and her appearance is inauspicious. A man starting on a journey will postpone it if he catches sight of a widow as he sets out, and the good widow will shrink back when she meets or crosses a man's path for fear of being the harbinger of evil to him. If she has borne no children to her husband, she is burned without the rites of religion. It is, perhaps, necessary to explain specifically that all these things tend to her spiritual exaltation.

A middle-aged widow who has borne children can manage to support this degraded existence. If she is the mother of a son, a sort of clemency is extended to her, for she has performed the first, and immeasurably the greatest, duty of Indian womanhood. Only by his son, begotten in lawful wedlock, performing certain exequial rites and ceremonies can a father be delivered from one of the Hindu hells; failure to bear a son is a first cause for introducing a second wife into the husband's house. A widow who has borne only daughters may find comfort in them. But the child-widow, whose husband has died when she was, perhaps, only six or seven years old, and to whom it was impossible to fulfil the prime duty of a wife—for her is reserved the cruelest and most unjust treatment of any. She is peculiarly repugnant to the community, one to whom no consideration or pardon can be extended, but only the unreasonable and unremitting hatred and abuse of her husband's people. For widowhood is regarded as a punishment for the sins committed by the woman, and the failure to bear a son is the Sin Unpardonable.

It is difficult to imagine anything more tragical or pathetic than the unfolding of this fate to the child-widow. She is too young to know what has happened, or only comprehends it very vaguely. She continues to play with her companions, for she is not called upon to enter the state of widowhood until she reaches the age of puberty. As a child, it makes little difference in her life, saving for a bitter word cast at her now and then, the reason for which she does not understand, or her hasty ejectment as a bad omen what time she may have unconsciously wandered into the proximity of a wedding-feast or some other festivity. But at length there comes a day when womanhood overtakes her, and she who never committed any sin has to suffer. The barber is called in, and her hair is shaved off; her bright clothes are taken away from her, and she is told that henceforth she must wear the sackcloth of mourning; her jewels, if she has any, are distributed amongst others; and she enters into a life of social ostracism. For what reason? For being the relict of a husband whose face she saw but once. More probably than not of a child-husband, and when you come to consider the statistics of mortality amongst children, you may gather some idea of the risk encountered by the Hindu bride when she enters into the state of matrimony!

Such a system and such treatment naturally lead to terrible results. Life becomes hopeless and intolerable, and frequently ends in suicide or enters into shame. In most cases, the child-widow has become the slave and drudge of the household; no work is too hard to impose upon her, and she is a stranger to any kindness or consideration. Probably she has a little more freedom than the wife is allowed, and there come to her temptations which may not be resisted. And if she succumbs to them, who can blame her?

Very frequently she falls into the clutches of the Brahmins, and is enjoined to make a pilgrimage to one of the holy cities to pray for her husband. The men of the temples are amorous, and the idols do not disdain young and pretty widows. It is natural for Hindu as for English widows to seek the solace of their religion. Bindraban is one of the holiest places of pilgrimage; there Krishna is worshipped, and to his shrine flock countless hosts of pilgrims, amongst them a vast number of widows. Here are the experiences and observations of one which have been recorded from her own lips.

"When we arrived at Bindraban, the priests of the place met us at the railway station, and got us a house, which was so filthy we could not endure it. We sought another, and found a good one belonging to a holy man. When he saw us women, he was very anxious for us to stay, but we knew what it meant, and left immediately. . . . The Brahmins' agents tell the widows, whom they seek in the villages and towns, that they will go to heaven if they proceed to these sacred places, and live there, and serve the priests, and worship the god Krishna. The poor ignorant women are easily persuaded to leave their homes, as many of them are very unhappy, and think it is far better to go and live and die in sanctuary, serving Krishna. Thus thousands of widows, young and old, go to Mathura or Bindraban, and fall into the snares of the priests. They soon expend the little they have in giving alms and presents to priests, and when all is spent, cannot return to their native land. Then, if they are tolerably young and good-looking, the holy men, saints, and religious mendicants are all after them, and get them to live in their houses, first as servants, then as mistresses. Or they hire them out to other men in the towns and villages. If the women are unwilling to lead immoral lives, they are told it is no sin to live thus in the service of Krishna. When they get old and displeasing to the men, they are turned out to shift for themselves, ragged, helpless, seemingly forsaken by all, and left to die like dogs. . . . We went round the town, and saw the condition of these women. There were thousands of widows, mostly from Bengal, and the heartless cruelty of man to woman, which we saw on every side, is almost beyond description."

Woman's wrongs are everywhere man's rights in India: the right to kill in infancy; the right to ruin; the right to coerce; the right to ill-treat. England has emancipated the African slave; her laws have protected the brute creation from cruelty. What is wanted in the twentieth century is a Wilberforce to rescue Indian womankind from her slavery, and a legislation to teach her lord and master the instincts of common humanity.

CHAPTER IX

THE INDIAN AT HOME

IT would require a thousand interviewers to report on "The Indian at Home" in all his phases. From the palace of the rajah to the hut of the ryot; from the furnished mansions of the Europeanised Parsees to the cave dwellings of some of the religious devotees; from the Swiss châlet-like cottages of the Himalayan mountaineers, perched high on craig, to the boats on the sea and river that give residence to an amphibious population; from the tents of the nomadic tribes in the deserts and the tree that shelters some of the pastoral races, to the crowded ant-nests of humanity in some of the city caravanserais,—from all these specimens of town and country life, city and jungle life, river and desert life, it is impossible to make a typical selection.

"There is safety in mediocrity," I was once informed by a Bengali baboo, who inclined to a middle course. And perchance a middle-class Hindu's house in Bengal will give us a sufficiently good idea of domestic life. I am beholden for my details to two or three Hindu gentlemen who have written on the subject.

The house is that of a well-to-do retired tradesman, let us say, who can afford to live comfortably. He is an elderly man, but his old crone of a mother is still alive, his four sons are all married, and have children, whilst two of his brothers and a son, deceased, have left widows, who, under the patriarchal system, all dwell under the same roof. It is a little commune, where the money earners contribute their wages to a common purse, from which the expenditure is apportioned by the head of the house, and where the womenfolk undertake all the domestic duties, with considerably more than their share foisted on the widows, except the old grandmother who rules in the *zenana*. Children tumble about promiscuously, and there is a general sensation of over-population within the walls. Privacy there is none, saving the fundamental privacy which partitions off the women's from the men's quarters.

The house stands in a garden, well cultivated, and containing a well or tank, and several shady trees. It is double storied, and the upper floor is reached by a cramped corkscrew staircase. The ground plan forms three sides of a square, with a courtyard in the centre, and the fourth side contains a *dállán*, or open reception-hall, which is a sort of general room, drawing-room (no ladies admitted), clubroom, schoolroom, and chapel. The most distinctive feature of the building are its verandahs. The interior is barn-like, owing to the absence of all furniture, and your first impression, as a European, is that of entering a disused house. One or two of the ground-floor rooms may be paved, but those upstairs are plastered with a coating of cow-dung over a layer of earth, as wood is not considered clean enough to eat off of. The walls are distempered, such a thing as wall-paper being unknown in India, where the damp of the rainy season would soon peel off that which the white ants spared. If you are permitted to peep into the *zenana*, in the absence of the inmates, you will see a little more decoration than in the men's quarters; but even here the most noticeable article is a commodious bed, and a few rude pictures painted on the walls are the only relief to the general suggestion of bareness. In lieu of chairs, there are small rugs or mats for the women to sit on, and the narrow windows are grated, not glazed. The whole interior is singularly dark and gloomy. There is no glass- or china-ware, brass taking their place, and you particularly observe the brass spittoons placed conspicuously about.

The *karta*, or head of the family, is a fat and elderly gentleman, whose costume consists of a single sheet wrapped round his waist, much as Englishmen adjust a bathing-towel on issuing from their tubs. We should call him a scandalously indecent old fellow, but you will find that all the men in the house adopt this principle of semi-nudity in their homes. Here, too, the turban is generally laid aside, and, needless to say, all the shoes have been left at the threshold, just as Europeans leave hats on a hall-stand. The *karta's* head is shaved, except for a tuft on the back centre of the poll; he wears a necklace of beads to assist him in his prayers, and a "sacred thread" girdles him from shoulder to waist, which is the insignia of his high caste. His brown naked skin shines from its polish of mustard oil, a very favourite application, and his chief employment is squatting on his hunkers and smoking a hookah.

The routine of household life is singularly simple. At the earliest sign of dawn, for all India is awake and stirring long before sunrise, the widows of the house come stealing down from the upper rooms to perform their ablutions, which, in the chilly morning air of the cold weather, consist of a perfunctory pouring of water over hands and face, to be followed by a bath later in the day. The sweeping and dusting of the house is a very simple operation, and where the floor is the common table, it is necessarily kept scrupulously clean. Then follows the milking of the cows and goats, for every one who can, keeps these in a country where milk takes the place of tea, coffee, cocoa, ale, wine, and spirits. The drawing of water also is no slight task where the household is a large one, but it is not necessary for washing purposes, as everybody goes to the well or tank for that purpose, and even the women bathe in the open, changing their wet garments for dry ones with such quickness and dexterity as to deceive the eye like a conjurer's trick.

By this time, the men of the house will be beginning to stir, and custom demands that the women should retire to their own part of the building. Dressing with the men is a simple affair, but their ablutions take a long time, being accompanied by an immense amount of teeth-washing and expectoration. Cleansed and purified, the worship of the household gods next demands attention. These are rather images than idols. In a niche of a room, squatting upon its own little altar, is the representation of the deity the family worship. In front of this, *puja* has to be made, and its precincts sprinkled with rice and flowers. There is more punctuality about family prayers in Bengal than in Britain, only ladies are not admitted. After this observance, hookahs are lighted, and the lords and masters while away the time until the womenfolk serve the morning meal, which is the principal one of the day.

In those houses where the expense can be afforded, a Brahmin is kept as cook, for any one can eat of what he has prepared, whilst if the women of the house do the cooking, only those of the same caste can be entertained. It requires no small amount of skill to obtain variety and tempt the appetite with the somewhat limited resources of a Hindu larder. You may enumerate the contents as ghee (rancid butter), oil, spices, vegetables, grain, and fish, which is a permissible diet, and almost a staple where a river or the sea is at hand. Allowing for the difference of taste, Hindu culinary science leaves crude British methods far behind. The possibilities of rice have never been suspected in England, where it is only imported to be barbarously treated, whereas, properly boiled, spiced, and flavoured, it has inherent capabilities not inferior to maccaroni. Cooking is a universal accomplishment in the East; amongst those who profess the art are *chefs* whose skill is exquisite, such for instance as the Mugs of Chittagong; but apart from the professional cook, "every schoolboy" can prepare his own dinner, and when in service every man is his own cook.

The Cengali's *menu* is varied, and his appetite enormous. Measure for measure, your Indian will far outstrip the European in eating capacity. On the floor, four or five large dishes and as many small ones figure, consisting of soup, fish, currie, rice, cakes, puddings, porridge, pulse, and fruit, but very different in their component parts from what the English are accustomed to under the same names, and in their order of serving.

Every one eats with his fingers. The women wait upon the men; withal very carefully, for each man has his own platter, and to touch it or him, even though it is his wife who does so, contaminates his food and renders it uneatable. Another peculiarity of caste is that no individual may leave his seat until all his fellows have finished their meal. Any food remaining uneaten has to be thrown away, or given to pariahs, human or canine. In some castes, it is essential for a man to bathe before partaking of food, and the meal is often required to be eaten in nudity, with merely a loin-cloth worn.

After the morning meal those who have occupation depart, not to eat again till nightfall, unless it be a few sweetmeats to stay the pangs of hunger. The master of the family, in such a household as I am describing, who has grown-up sons to carry on his business, will probably leave it to them, and pass his time till the heat of the day in smoking and chewing *pán*, which is a sort of "quid" indulged in inordinately by both men and women. It is composed of betel nut, spices, and lime, and the spittoons to which I have referred are a very necessary adjunct in a house. In the heat of the day, every Indian who can manage it indulges in a siesta. With the decline of the sun at three o'clock, the social hours begin, and the men wander forth to "eat the air." Pastimes, in the English sense of the word, the Hindu has few or none. He does not ride, shoot, or subject himself to any physical exertion; indeed, such is held to be derogatory. Fishing is an exception, and he is remarkably fond of the piscatorial art. He also plays cards or chess occasionally. But his chief pleasure consists in chattering and visiting, disputing and arguing, and if he has the chance of dissipation it is freely indulged in. His life is full of holidays, which have to be respected on religious grounds, and afford him much scope for the exercise of his lazy and dilettante idiosyncrasies.

Meanwhile, the women remain shut up in the seclusion of the domestic part of the house, but far from idle. The superintendence of the cooking is in itself a task that occupies a long time, and there are three meals to be served, one for the men, another for the children, and a third for the women themselves. They, too, must have their midday nap, and bathing and devotions cannot be neglected. Perhaps in the afternoon the Hindu lady finds a little spare time for visiting or receiving a visit from her women friends, and even playing a game of cards. Later on, she makes her toilette, and although compliments or admirers can never come her way, she bestows great attention upon her dress and ornaments, and daily smears her forehead with the patch of vermilion that denotes her married state. In the evening, there may be a story-teller, an old woman eloquent with ancient legend, called in to make an hour pass, but you will find no such things as books, musical instruments, sketching materials, or the ordinary diversions and distractions one is accustomed to associate with womankind in her boudoir. The Bengali lady's costume, it may be noted, consists of one piece of cloth wound round her body in a way to cover it, but it hardly serves to conceal the symmetry, and the thin muslins in fashion often render it indecorous. In those parts of India where the Mahomedan influence has made itself most felt, the women wear trousers, which are always fashioned of coloured cloth in contradistinction to the men's, which are seldom anything but white. A more hideous garment than the woman's *pyjama* probably does not exist. But the Bengali lady is very classically draped, and sometimes presents a most voluptuous sight.

The evening brings supper and the preparations for it, and this is the concluding function of the day. There is no recreation afterwards, for as it is early to rise, so it is early to bed. Indeed, in the ill-lighted Hindu house, any recreation, except conversation, after dark is practically impossible.

The home-life of the peasant presents a more primitive picture. The distinction of a *zenana* is beyond his means, or, more probably, not necessary in his caste. His home is a hut, containing a single room, the walls of mud, the roof thatched, and the interior as bare as a barn. In the plains country, he lives in a village in which the houses cluster together, a survival of the old predatory days of rapine and foray, when men had to gather in communities in order to protect themselves, and many a field was ploughed and many a harvest gathered under an armed guard. Even now the custom has survived of enclosing villages within a wall, making each a miniature stronghold. Around them stretch the cultivated lands and fields, not divided by hedges and ditches, but apportioned off in tiny plots, intermingling with one another, their boundaries defined by low earth banks. A man may possess half an acre cut up into half a dozen such plots, and interspersed with the holdings of others, like the black and white squares on a chess-board.

The peasant rises early and performs his ablutions, and in this respect the native of India might set an example to his agricultural brother in more civilised lands, for he laves himself with water very frequently. He is off early to the fields, taking some cold food with him to break his fast. At noon, his wife brings him his dinner, which is generally followed by a sleep. From three till sunset, he is again at the plough or whatever work is in progress. Ploughing is the only operation not shared in by the women, who, in addition to helping their husbands in the fields, perform all the household work. If the fine *zenana* lady has cause to complain of time hanging heavily on her hands, her humbler sister cannot. Apart from her domestic duties, there is water to be brought in, often entailing a long journey, and fuel to be provided. The working up of cow-dung into what are familiarly known as "cakes" for fuel, and plastering them on the side of the hut to dry in the sun, absorb no inconsiderable portion of her time; or, maybe, wood has to be cut and carried from the distant jungle if the house is in a timbered district. At the busy seasons, you may see the woman working whilst her husband is enjoying his siesta, and it is rarely that any time is restful for her. She knows, too, what it is to be hungry whilst her husband is satisfied, and the pride and satisfaction of "dressing the baby" can never be hers, whose children are habitually naked.

The thriftiness of the peasant is marvellous. I have often seen the women sweeping the little *khêts*, or fields of rice, with a hand-broom after harvest to collect the fallen grain, and gathering singly those ears that happen to have ripened before the bulk of the crop. In the mango season, it is not an uncommon thing to suspend one meal because sustenance can be derived from the wild fruit. And, for waste, the care with which grain just sufficient for a meal, no more and no less, is estimated, indicates a mind as calculating as it is frugal. And this grain, be it noted, except in Bengal and other favoured rice-growing districts, is rarely rice, which is far too much of a luxury for the peasant's fare. His ordinary food consists of millet, pulse, and other coarse grain, with salt and chillies for a condiment.

Cattle have been called the peasant's children, and next only to himself is his heed for them. If you wanted to express the ryot's idea of perfect prosperity, you have only to add a yoke of oxen to the three acres and a cow which were once held out as a lure to the English agricultural voter.

There are millions of peasants in India who exist on half an acre, and whose cattle for eight months in the year are little removed from walking skeletons. In Australia, they allow an acre for each sheep; were it possible to allow the same in India for the human being, the standard of comfort would be considerably increased.

The native of India has one capacity which more civilised people do not possess. He can make himself at home anywhere, and adapt himself to all sorts and conditions of places. Away from his own home, he experiences no trouble about lodging. He will "fix up" anyhow. His bed is a blanket, which he invariably carries with him; his impedimenta a water-vessel and a pan to cook his food in. His apartment is a circle swept clear and clean on the bare earth, under a tree for choice. Except in the colder latitudes, where a tent is necessary, there is no need to make any arrangements for servants when travelling or camping out. They turn in like dogs; on the floor of a verandah, at the door of your tent, in the stable, under a tree, or sheltered by the bullock cart that is carrying your equipage. On the highways of India, you will see under almost every shady tree the ashes of burnt-out fires, which represent the camping-grounds of wayfarers. In towns and cities, there are places called "serais," where the charge for accommodation varies from a halfpenny to fourpence a night, but they are merely open sheds, and many a native prefers to save his halfpenny and camp under the walls outside. When the crops are ripening, the peasant erects a *machán*, or elevated squatting place, in the middle of his fields, and remains on the watch all night to scare away the deer, jackals, wild pig, and other predatory animals that loot his crops. A man will make a pilgrimage that takes him many weeks, and never pay a farthing for lodging all the time. Many of the pastoral tribes have no roof, except the vault of heaven.

In city life, the case is very different, and the many-storied human warrens of such places as Calcutta and Bombay can only be likened to ants' nests. In a native city like Lucknow or Hyderabad, where the Mahomedan element predominates, and the seclusion of all the women is necessary, the overcrowding transcends the Jews' quarters in Whitechapel. Under such conditions, caste, and even custom, have to give way to convenience, or, at least, what is practicable, and domestic privacy in its rural state becomes impossible except for the wealthy. For rents have to be paid, and that is a very disagreeable form of expenditure in a land where, although the population is as poor as the proverbial church mouse, yet it is a fact that more than four fifths of the people pay no rent, but live in their own houses!

To summarise the Indian home, you may say that it affords shelter from the sun and rain, and supplies that amount of privacy which walls can afford. But when you seek for comfort, taste, and decoration, you seek in vain. In its social aspect, it is entirely wanting in that spirit which lends enchantment to our own idea of home life, and leaves us little cause to regret that in his selfishness and suspicion the native of India is practically always "not at home" to callers.

CHAPTER X

IN THE SUNSHINE

"ARE you happy?"

"I am happy."

That is one of the commonest forms of salutation in the East, corresponding to our "How d' you do?"—"Quite well, thank you." But the conventional inquiry and stereotyped reply mean little. "I am happy," a man answered me once, with a very lugubrious face, who, I learned on further questioning, had lost nine of his nearest and dearest relations from cholera during the three preceding days.

I am conscious that so far in this attempt to depict daily life in India the colours used have been sombre. It has been unavoidable, for India is a land of penury and privation, struggle and starvation, woe and want, for the vast majority. England is not "merrie" when times are hard; in India, the times are always more or less hard. A popular handbook tells us that the Indian peasant is at the best of times not far from the verge of starvation, and the statement is not exaggerated.

I harp on the peasant, but, after all, he is nine tenths of the country.

Let us see what sunshine there is in the lives of the native Indians over and above that superabundance poured upon the land, what are their theories of enjoying themselves, their amusements, their diversions, and recreations. Prosperity and happiness are often synonymous terms, and I think material prosperity yields more unalloyed delight in the East than in the West. There is much of the miser in the native of India, and the accumulation of money, or its equivalent, brings rapture to the brown soul. The money-lender's ledger is a book whose perusal brings him more pleasure than all the other literature of the East. I have seen a spiritual gleam of happiness on the face of a shepherd, whose features were ordinarily as witless as those of his own sheep and goats, what time the lambing season came round, and things were going well. And I have often observed a peasant squatting on one of the banks that divided his fields, contemplating his ripening crops with a smile that intimated sunshine in his soul. The happiest ryot I ever knew was a landless labourer, who, after twenty years of frugality and self-denial, saved sufficient to buy himself an acre of land. I vow that man was a monument of merriness; his face always engendered a sympathetic grin in mine; it made one happy by infection to look at him. "Happy! Bigly happy!" was his spontaneous ejaculation every time I met him.

But this, after all, does not describe the sort of sunshine the chapter-heading aims at, which rather refers to moral than material cheerfulness. The basis of happiness in England is home life; if a man is happy at home, it makes up for all the kicks he gets abroad. How about the home life of the native of India?

His ideas of domesticity are very foreign to ours, and it is difficult to enter into his feelings. Where he has sons I think probably you can account him content. A son is something more to him than one to the Emperor of Austria or the Tzar of Russia, for a male child is necessary to his salvation in a future state. A great light beams on his house when a son is born. As for his wife, she is quite a secondary consideration; she can be replaced, but a son cannot be assured. I remember sympathising with a native friend, quite a superior man, whose wife and son were both dangerously ill. He was filled with anguish for the latter, but when I ventured a guarded inquiry (as etiquette demanded) about the former, "*Kúch perwáni!*" was the reply—"No matter about her."

The native is a fond parent, often a doting one. He systematically spoils his children. Even a daughter, whose advent is dreaded, will worm her way into her father's heart. There was another native friend of mine I used to visit periodically who always had a bed brought out for me to sit on, and placed in the shade of a tree in front of his house. By-and-by, as I became a familiar figure, his little daughter would shyly steal out to reconnoitre the *sahib*, and, growing bolder, nestle in her father's lap, and proceed to tease him. The thing told its own tale, and I cannot conceive that man was anything but happy in his domestic relation with that daughter. And when she married at the age of twelve, and left his home for good, I often used to think he missed the childish caresses, which he accepted before me with such an air of apologetic shamefacedness, from a loving little girl who would not be denied her demonstration of affection. And I should certainly say that the girl-child, so unwelcome at her birth, had come to be a ray of sunshine—whilst it lasted—in her father's life.

The inaccessibility of an Indian home makes it impossible for the European to form any trustworthy opinion of its constitutional happiness or otherwise. Hindu writers insist on its joys, and, while admitting the harsh conditions under which they live, declare the womenfolk are contented and happy. This may be true, but it is seldom, if ever, indicated in the external behaviour or the appearance of the females, which rather create the idea of a subdued melancholy. But for the men, I readily admit that affection for "home" in the abstract is a feature in their characters; but I should hesitate before I committed myself as to whether it is for the place or the people in it. It is a difficult topic to touch on in conversation with a native, who never "lets himself out" on this aspect of his life.

Coming to the amusements of the people, you find them singularly crude. There are no national games, save those the English have introduced through the medium of schools. Cricket and football amongst the schoolboys of the modern rising generation are now common enough, but they are only played by the educated youth, and that in India is the equivalent of what the conditions in England would be if the great public schools monopolised those sports. All the world over, children will play, but they have fewer toys to play with in India than in any land I know of, and leave off playing sooner in life than elsewhere, and, as they marry early, grow staid early. I remember talking to a Mahomedan youth twelve years of age, the son of a Nawab, who was going to England to be educated at Harrow. He was married earlier than usual in life for a Mahomedan, because he would be absent when the proper time arrived, and his father wanted the match secured. He was the most precocious boy I ever conversed with, entered into a description of his home life, told me his step-mother was very jealous of him and he always went in fear that she would poison him, described his bride and criticised her want of accomplishments, and protested that he spent his leisure in reading *Sadi* and the Koran. An Englishman of double his age would not have talked more seriously and soberly, and for his deportment, it was that of a grown-up person. In my plantation I employed a great number of boys from ten or eleven to fifteen or sixteen years of age, and I can never call to mind seeing them playing out of work-hours.

The Indian *Tamásha*, or entertainment and amusement combined, is one where a few perform and the many look on. Festivals are far more numerous than in England, but (except in the case of fairs, with which I shall deal presently) frolic enters only into one. The annual *Déwali* festival is a saturnalia of horse-play and indecency, during which the mild and staid Hindu seems to lose his head utterly. He expends his energies in sousing everybody he meets with red water and yellow powder to a chorus of "*Holi*, *holi*, *holi*," and a commentary of obscene jests and jokes. At certain other festivals, he goes in for gambling. But his general idea of a Bank Holiday has physical laziness at the back of it, and a good long sleep or bask in the sun, smoking his hookah, affords him all the relaxation and enjoyment he seeks.

Horse-racing is unknown to him; cricket and football he does not understand; rowing is the privilege of a caste, being a calling; theatres he has none; the pleasures of a walk for walking's sake are outside his comprehension; "courting" is against his custom; reading is beyond his powers. If I were asked to summarise his idea of thoroughly amusing himself, I should say sight-seeing. He wants something to look at, not something to do. He dislikes manly sports and hobbies he has none. The idea of a native training for physical proficiency, or bicycling for pleasure, or pigsticking, or taking up photography, or going in for botany, or collecting anything for art's sake, is too remote to be considered. What are the sports of the great and the rich? Nautch-girls and music, cock-fighting and pitting wild animals one against the other, hunting with a cheetah, or falconry. A few shoot, but from the ease of an elephant's howdah, or for the "pot." Ask them to walk up a marsh for snipe and they will think you mad. To aim at a flying bird is accounted folly by the native shikari.

Nor is the native capable of deriving any pleasure from the beauties of nature. A pretty scene, a lovely sunset, an artistic blend of colours lack the power of appealing to him. His nosegays are red and yellow; his finest artists have not the remotest idea of depicting a landscape; he will look at an English picture upside down. Music he enjoys, but it is the sort of music that sends a European distracted. He is not ordinarily tickled by a joke, and he laughs little, and never loudly. There is a certain sour dignity in his code of etiquette which debars him from romping with children, or indulging in any physical pastime, and this repression is extended to those feelings the exhibition of which indicates pleasure with Europeans.

Women are naturally more restricted than men in their pleasures and amusements. Even in the *zenanas* of the rich, books merely mention their love of dress and jewellery, as constituting their chief pleasure, and story-telling and a game of cards are their principal amusements. The recreations of the lower orders are even fewer, and perhaps their most enjoyable hour is that when the gathering round the well to draw water permits the luxury of a gossip, which they thoroughly appreciate.

Without doubt, feasting affords the greatest general gratification. It is the leading form of entertainment. To feast the Brahmins is particularly enjoined in the sacred books of the Hindus, and no ceremony or festival is complete without a banquet. Beggars congregate on such occasions with the knowledge they will not go away empty. In nine cases out of ten, when your native asks you for leave of absence, it is to attend some *burra khána*, or big dinner. Backslidings from caste invariably require the giving of a feast to secure forgiveness and purification. In a land where hunger is chronic, and death from starvation periodical, it is easy to understand that a full stomach may mean the acme of joy. No native feeds oftener than twice a day, and in some cases only once. They have prodigious powers of eating, and I have known men lament their Gargantuan appetite as a handicap on their livelihood, and put it forward as a plea for extra pay. On the other hand, there is a species of rice which is very expensive, and only purchased by the wealthy, because (as was explained to me) it is easily digested, and you get hungry again within two hours. The term "prosper and wax fat" has its many illustrations in India, where a man's worldly circumstances may be correctly gauged by his circumference. Fatness is a charm in women, and a cause for envy in men; *khub moti* (beautifully fat) is a common phrase of compliment. Eastern life is sensual, and the appetite of the stomach not the least source of pleasure. What drinking is in the West, that is eating in the East; the medium of self-indulgence and conviviality.

I should also feel inclined to rank idleness as one of the chief delights of the Indian. "The apathetic attitude of contemp'ative Asia" has been made familiar to us in books of travel, but I do not think we quite realise what pure enjoyment there is in some of that apathy. The native is an adept in the art of doing nothing; it never bores him to be idle; on the contrary, he seems to take a positive pleasure in prolonging his inaction, and will squat on his hams by the hour, like a crow on a wall, and enjoy it as much as Western people do reading a novel in an easy armchair, or listening to a concert. I would even go so far as to say of the average native that he is seldom so happy as when he is idle; and outside the islands of the Pacific I doubt if you will find a more devoted disciple of the *dolce far niente*. The educated mind and the active body of the mentally and physically energetic Briton may make him scout such a contention, but feed the Anglo-Saxon on vegetable diet for three generations, plant him in a tropical climate, eliminate from his resources the ability to read, and reduce his surroundings to those which are within reach of the native, and I fancy he would begin to discover unsuspected possibilities of enjoying himself in the passive.

There is one species of amusement which stands out in the economy of Indian life as universal and supreme, and that is the *méla*, or fair. It may be a religious festival in honour of some shrine, or a great annual gathering like that of Hurdwar, or a purely commercial business like the cattle-fairs held in various parts of India, but it represents the native's most extended idea of dissipation. For weeks before, it is the one subject of his anticipation; for weeks after, the one topic of his conversation. It is the single species of festivity in which the women have almost as great a part as the men; not, of course, the poor *zenana* captives, who are never let out of their prisons, but the ordinary native woman who leaves her home for a holiday as seldom as the omnibus-driver does his box. To them, the fair is what the Christmas pantomime is to children who are taken to the theatre once a year; their glee is childish, and to be forbidden the treat would certainly reduce them to tears.

An Indian fair is a far more picturesque scene

than an English one, and none held in England can compete with even a moderate gathering out in the East. As the population of India is numbered in hundreds of millions and that of Great Britain in tens of millions, so it is with the vast and overwhelming multitudes that attend these fairs. They gather together such crowds as nothing short of a Coronation or Jubilee can collect in England. To English eyes, the most extraordinary part of the spectacle is the sudden apparition of more women than you ever suspected were in the land; one wonders where they all spring from, and marvels that so much comeliness should remain hidden, if it is lawful to be seen. But there is a sort of license allowed to women in attending a fair, and for once in a way, all their faces are smiling instead of decorous. You may live many years in India and form the opinion that the women are—I will not say ugly, but decidedly unattractive. Go to a fair, and the revelation bursts on you that they can hold their own in looks with any country in the world. Perhaps it is the unaccustomed smile that lights up their features—usually prudish and stand-offish in the ordinary episodes of life. And yet, no; I can call to mind *mêlas* in the hill-country, where the lighter complexioned races live, which left me with a suspicion that, after all, the Anglo-Saxon woman might not be so beautiful as the Aryan. And one thing is certain about these fairs: they serve to bring out the fair. I do not mean an abominable pun by that, but the simple statement of fact that you see at them a vast number of women who are not daily exposed to the sun, and realise that the women of India are far lighter complexioned than the men.

And then their dresses! The fashion may be two thousand years old, but the wealth of colour, the tinsel, the prodigality of silver jewellery taken in the mass present such a *coup d'œil* as would make Ascot or Goodwood look comparatively colourless. It is as an Autumn sunset shining upon Autumn leaves, all warm and glowing, with the glint of running water counterfeited in the abundant silver necklaces, hair-ornaments, bangles, and anklets. The display of jewellery, which assumes a snobbish aspect with the English, never seems excessive in the native woman. I have seen her laden with it, and yet could never think to myself, "You would look far better if you left half of those ornaments at home!" There is no "snobbishness" in the Indian, except in the case of the Europeanised native.

The fun of an Indian fair is noisy and demonstrative; the merry-go-round is a feature of it, and the music is of the loudest. There are the Oriental equivalents of all the itinerant entertainers to which one is accustomed in the West, and the trash offered for sale is quite equal to that purchased at a charity bazaar. As a rule, every one has money to spend, for all have been saving up for this day for months past and temptation to spend it is spread around. A nation which "thinks in cowrie shells" (whereof a hundred go to a penny) can probably make sixpence go farther than any other, and enjoy the going of it more than a people to whom the patronage of a penny-in-the slot machine means a bagatelle and not a day's wage expended. The slot-machines of India would have to be manufactured to respond to cowrie shells.

I have altogether forgotten fireworks, which are a distinct item in the list of native amusements. The evenings are cool, fine nights can be discounted, and the form of entertainment is one you can enjoy sitting at your ease on the ground. That meets every requirement of the East, and fireworks are one of the most popular forms of amusement. Illuminations, too, must be mentioned; to a people accustomed to live in the dark after nightfall, such exhibitions have a special delight, and the Indian *chirág*, or oil-lamp, especially adapts itself to the occasion.

If a contented mind is a continual feast, it should take little to make the native happy, for so little contents him, and his horizon is small. He tires slowly of a toy, and in this his otherwise childish capacity for enjoyment contrasts with the easily tired nature of English children. He will listen to the same tune, look at the same performance repeated over and over again, without any apparent diminution of satisfaction. Music and mirth are too rare in his life to bore him easily.

He cannot have too much of a good thing, and his entertainments are seldom affairs of less than twelve hours.

I have left to the last perhaps the most typical, as it certainly is the most contradictory, example of the "sunshine of life" in India. Were I asked which was the happiest moment of any year to the average native, I would say, without hesitation, the one in which the sky was dark and threatening—the breaking of the monsoon. There is no music in India like that of falling rain in May or June; no sunshine, literal or metaphorical, that can bring such joy as the clouds which sweep up from the south-west. What the rising of the Nile is to the Egyptian fellah, that and something more is the breaking of the rainy season to the ryots. Out they come tumbling from huts and hovels at the first pitter-patter of the great drops, their grateful eyes lifted to the skies, and the pæan of thankfulness, "*Rám, Rám, Mahadeo!*" bursting from their lips. Here is salvation, here not the happiness of a passing hour, but security for the whole year. I have myself in that arid land felt something of the thrill that follows the falling of rain after a long, hot drought, and for the poor peasant—well, it may be a paradox, a contradiction in terms, but the weeping rain-clouds bring the greatest amount of sunshine into his life.

CHAPTER XI

THE GOLDEN EAST

WE call the East golden and India the brightest jewel in the British Crown. Let us examine physical and practical facts a little more closely, and see whether figurative fancies are founded on them.

The East is so far golden that it is certainly a land of sunshine. You can predict a fine day six months, or, for the matter of that, six years ahead. Theoretically, you can also predict a rainy one, but the clouds are not so consistent as the sunshine. The rainy season sometimes belies its name, and then comes famine. In England people grumble at meteorological conditions; curse the unwelcome rain, protest against a three weeks' drought, and have fault to find with fogs and east winds. But, with the exception of a few bronchial folk, these climatic freaks do not kill; one is not dependent on the skies for life and fortune. The Indian is. Two inches of rain withheld in its due season will destroy more human life than a quarter of a century of European warfare, and cause as much human suffering as Bonaparte did in his career.

A very worthy Kentish farmer was grumbling to me one day because the rainy summer had ruined his hops, half ruined his corn, and damaged his hay. "Are your wife and children alive?" I asked him. He replied, with some surprise, in the affirmative. "Your horses seem pretty sleek?" I observed. He admitted they were in capital condition. "And your cows?" Ah, they had done well, the pasturage was good. "Poultry?" The wife looked after them, and she had not complained. "You have not been compelled to shut up your house, and leave it to look after itself whilst you emigrated?" He thought I was a lunatic. "But you say this is the very worst season that any man ever suffered?" Of that he was perfectly sure; he had not paid his rent, and some of the wages bill would have to come out of his pocket. "Well," I said, "if you had been an Indian farmer, and this had been the worst season that any man ever suffered from, your wife, children, horses, stock, and poultry would all be dead, and, presuming you had been so lucky as to escape with your life, you would be handling a shovel on relief works on the west coast of Ireland." "Gor! Get out," he said.

But the analogy is absolutely correct, and the possibility of such an experience threatens millions of homes every year in India in that acute and critical time when the rainy season is due.

For India may be golden in legend, but is not a fruitful garden land in fact. Take it, square mile for square mile, and it is infinitely more barren than fertile. Outside the favoured zones, it is, in places populously inhabited, less fruitful than Scotland, whilst vast areas are waterless desert and sandy waste. You may pass in a railway-carriage for hour after hour through long tracts of country, where the spiritless vegetation and the bare rocky hills appal, and see "crops" you would think only fit to plough into the ground.

British ideas of India are often gathered from those rich coastal districts which they first settled, narrow zones for the most part, or fertile river basins like Bengal. But India away from its rivers and its cloud-catching mountains is a dry, drear land, and the popular conception of its tropic prodigality is completely erroneous. It is so barren of timber, for instance, that the soil is deprived of the fertilising elements it requires by the universal use of cattle manure for fuel, and so dry that the fields have to be irrigated by the primitive process of the Persian wheel, where a man on a treadmill doles the water out of a well in quarts to dribble it over his fields in cupfuls.

Nor are the elements man's only enemy. Pestilence and plague scourge him, and fever, insidiously but surely, kills more every year than famine. A great cholera-wave or a plague visitation startles people, and arrests the attention by the suddenness or magnitude of its holocaust. But of fever, infinitely the greatest death-dealer in India, comparatively nothing is heard. With its alternate shivering and burning fits, that rack the system, it is as common in many places as influenza in England. You see a man huddled up on the ground, shaking and groaning, and hardly trouble to ask "What 's the matter?" "Oh, it 's only fever," comes the stereotyped reply. The disease is too common to cause the slightest surprise or evoke the crudest compassion. The victim must go through his bout. He is left on the ground, and, when the fit is over, gets up and goes about his work, and continues to do so until the system is worn out or a cold contracted, and he "snuffs out." No inconsiderable portion of the mortality in India is "snuffing out." Sickness is bad enough in England, where there is a doctor in every community, but in India, where at least two hundred million persons cannot get one unless they are prepared to walk or be carried to the dispensary, which may be twenty or fifty miles away, sickness is the half-way house to death.

I have mentioned the word plague, and the reader has probably associated it with the bubonic plague; but there are other plagues in Indian life similar to those which the Egyptians suffered. Wild beasts and venomous reptiles enter into the economy of daily life with a shocking freedom. Of savage wild beasts, such as the tiger and wolf,

I will not pause to write; they are too well known by repute. But many a peasant s life is rendered a burden to him by wild pig, deer, jackals, and monkeys. Where a man is dependent on the produce of an acre for his sustenance for a year, any of the above can dock his commissariat considerably. The mere driving of them away constitutes a serious tax on his time. When crops are ripening, it means a month of wakeful nights, perched upon a platform on poles stuck in his field, and I have often been aroused in camp in a wooded country by the voice of the sleepy watcher hooting at four-footed depredators through the night. And this brings me to another reflection. How happy would the British agricultural labourer be if deer and game were common in their fields and open to any one to slay and eat! Most parts of India swarm with game; hare, partridge, and quail abound round every village; many cultivated areas are devastated by deer, antelope, and wild pig; there are few jungles which do not harbour pea-fowl and jungle-fowl, and scarce a sheet of water but holds teal and wild-duck. But the Indian peasant, unless he is a hunter by caste, seldom disturbs them, and the men who starve on a diet of pulse and millet take no advantage of the sumptuous feast of venison and game which can be had for the snaring. In some cases, of course, it may be against their caste to eat flesh, but in numerous instances it is not, and I can only ascribe to the native's listless apathy this rejection of plenty thrown in his path. He sadly wants a few lessons in the finer phases of the art of poaching. Here, at least, Nature is bountiful to him, and he takes no advantage of her bounty!

Snakes, scorpions, and centipedes are amongst the inconveniences of native life, and where the population goes about with naked feet, the risk is much greater than with the booted European. Few Hindus will, however, kill a snake, and the foul reptile lives and deals death unscathed. I have seen a man guide one out of his path with a stick to the accompaniment of apologetic *salaams* and prayers, and I have been besought on bended knee not to discharge my gun at one at which it was levelled! To the lesser pests of life, flies, sand-flies, mosquitoes, *et hoc genus*, the native seems impervious, but he endures much tribulation from vermin of an unpleasant nature.

In a country where vegetarianism is adopted by most of the people, you would think the art of fruit and vegetable growing would be brought to a high pitch. But such is not the case. The native palate in this respect is terribly coarse—I am talking of the commonalty—and assimilates unripe fruit and indigestible roots with content, not to say gusto. Strong-flavoured turnips and radishes are the varieties chiefly vended, and leaf products which are equivalent to spinach, but lacking its delicacy of flavour. Two or three of the indigenous vegetables commend themselves to English taste, but the majority are such as we would toss to our cattle and sheep. Few countries in the world can grow more delicious fruit than India, and those varieties you purchase in the markets of Calcutta or Bombay, where the European and wealthy native demand has made their cultivation and development profitable, are things to dream about. But they are Covent Garden luxuries to what is obtainable in the country at large. The peasant's mango bears the same relation to the luscious fruit of Bombay as the crab-apple to the Ribstone pippin, and the plantain of the up-country bazaar is appropriately named the "horse-plantain."

Meat in India is as bad as it can scarcely fail to be in a parched land were you have to kill it and eat it the same day. The favourite flesh of the native is goat, which is like a very rank, sapless, sinewy mutton. The Mahomedans eat beef, but in the Hindu centres, the killing of kine is prohibited by law. Butter and milk are poor in quality, but goat's milk may be accounted an exception. The water is universally bad, and, in those localities where "tank" or pond water has to be used, too vile and contaminated to be described. The contents of a London third-class swimming-bath would be as distilled in comparison.

Food grains, except some of the better classes of wheat and rice, are inferior. The sowing of mixed crops in the same field, and the crude methods of reaping, threshing with cattle treading out the straw, and winnowing—every operation conducted on the surface of the bare earth—make the bulk dirty and full of foreign substances. The quality, too, of some of the commoner sorts of rice renders it unfit for European consumption. Probably not more than a third of the natives of India eat rice as a regular diet; the majority exist on unleavened cakes, called *chuppattis*, made from flour of inferior grains. These cakes are circular in shape, leathery in consistency, and flavourless. They require a relish, and have given rise to the chutnies and condiments associated with Indian dietary, which are the apotheosis of the crude relishes peculiar to the different countries of the Empire.

Sweetmeats hold a high place, and the sweetmeat shops in the bazaar present a pleasing variety and ingenuity, but the *ghee*, or rancid butter, which enters into their composition renders an appreciation of them by the English palate impossible. Of the intoxicating drinks, the use of which has increased under British rule, there is not one, with the exception of newly drawn "toddy," that does not merit the usual epithet of "rank poison." They are chiefly consumed by the lower classes, opium being the aristocratic intoxicant of the East. In India, it is swallowed, not smoked, as in China, and is the daily vice of countless slaves to the habit. The smoking of *bhang*, or Indian hemp, is very common amongst some orders; it is the most deleterious of drugs, producing a state akin to *delirium tremens*, and as a factor in crime takes the place of drink in England. Amongst the wealthier classes, European wines and spirits are commonly consumed, though it may be on the sly, and champagne backed with brandy is the tipple of many rajahs.

Crime and litigation give plenty of work in the law courts, where three million civil suits and two million criminal cases are disposed of annually, or, respectively, one in a hundred and one in a hundred and fifty of the population—a very high average. But the native character finds a positive charm in litigation. If lawyers do not grow fat in India, it is only because there are so many of them. They are as wolfish as the usurers, and, after them, the principal cause of the impoverishment of the people. A vast revenue is raised by stamps, every approach to the bench of justice having to be made on stamped paper, and court fees are one of the heaviest items of litigation. Although it is unprofessional, a great number of native lawyers tout for clients, and as a body they are a grabbing lot.

You do not require gold to pay wages in the Golden East, where silver is the currency, and bank or "currency" notes the convenient monetary medium in common use. These notes vary from seven and eightpence in value to very large amounts, and become, in process of circulation, almost as "microbic" as the coppers of the country. Sixteen is the principal numerical factor; sixteen annas make a rupee, sixteen rupees a gold mohur, and it enters into some of the weights and measures. The sixteen-times multiplication table is one of the stumbling-blocks that have to be surmounted.

The mention of wages suggests that a list of those I paid in a prosperous tea-planting district of India may not be without its information. The able-bodied men received six and eightpence a month, common coolies five and fourpence, women four and eightpence, and useful boys four shillings, in all cases with huts to live in, but no other perquisites, and, of course, without food. Men in superior positions, such as gangers and overseers, drew from eight to sixteen shillings, and the head-carpenter was a comparative Crœsus on twelve pounds a year. When I first started, in the 'seventies, the "English writer," or clerk, was paid two pounds a month, but twenty-five years later, I could get the work done by better educated "Baboos" for little more than half that salary. For less than three pounds a month I engaged a "Doctor Baboo," who had passed through the medical schools at one of the universities, and was a qualified medical practitioner—"qualified to kill," some one unkindly suggested! The native engineer who had charge, and drove a tolerable amount of machinery, was paid two pounds a month. All these figures take the rupee at its present exchange value.

These may seem small wages, but "they can live on half their pay, and save the other half," said my head overseer to me one day when we were discussing matters. And then he explained how a man on five and fourpence a month expended sixteen-pence on thirty-two pounds of rice, which served him for a supper for as many days, eightpence on thirty pounds of Indian corn, which provided a good midday meal, and eightpence on such luxuries as salt, *ghee*, condiments, and lamp-oil; total, two shillings and eightpence, on which expenditure those men kept themselves in hard-working condition, able to do ten hours' hoeing in a stiff clay soil, a task from which most English labourers would have shied off; and for carrying burdens no English porter could have competed with them. I have frequently despatched a man with a load of sixty or seventy pounds weight on a twenty-four mile journey, and he did it, both literally and, in English slang, "on his head"—carrying the burden I allude to.

It may be said that the Indians as a nation are as much boggled in debt as the Government of Turkey or some of the South American Republics, and with as little chance of paying off their liabilities. The rate of interest in India is usually twenty-four per cent., sometimes twelve, very rarely nine, and frequently thirty and thirty-six. The banks habitually charge the up-country European ten per cent. It is a curious thing that the native, perhaps the most thrifty, prudent, and economical man in the world after the Chinese, should be utterly reckless in borrowing and litigation. A portion of his neediness arises no doubt from want, owing to bad seasons; but in that case he goes to the shopkeeper, who, although a grasping individual, is moderation compared to the extortion of the usurer. It is for his ceremonial expenses, his marryings and his funerals, that the native runs into debt headlong and blindly. The curse of custom compels him to this, for it insists he shall be lavish. The debt, too, is regarded as one of honour, and although he may willingly seek to repudiate or wriggle out of a commercial obligation, his code demands that he shall not deny the liability incurred for the execution of a religious duty. Moreover, for a man who thinks in shell coinage, it is difficult to attempt to shuffle out of a situation which requires him to expend in one week a sum equal to many years' income; his very character is bound up in the glory of that reckless week; it would never do to say it had cost him only five or six pounds when all the world had assessed the expenditure necessary on such festivities at ten or twenty.

If he has land, the peasant can always raise a loan, but seldom if ever comes the season when the land can repay it. And the usurer who holds the mortgage-deed has the law court to go to, that fount of British justice which will place him in possession of his own, as it has done. "Under the British Government the land in India has, to a large extent, passed away from the cultivator," writes Sir George Wingate, with the weight of authority. "In Assam, sixty-eight, and in the North-west Provinces, nearly forty-eight per cent. of the landlords are of the money-lending class. In the Punjab, the change is fraught with grave political danger."

The despotism of usury is weighing heavily on the Golden East. Under native rule, these things adjusted themselves in the throes of periodical change, and the absence of smooth-working legal machinery. But under the *Pax Britannica*, too many scoundrels, who prey upon the ignorant and poor, come by other people's property which they claim as their own on the strength of a liability much more than half of which is accrued compound interest. The place of the predatory Pindaris of the past, who lived by foray and rapine, has been taken by the money-lender and the lawyer, and these latter are the blood-sucking vampires who have battened on the want and witlessness of a population sunk in ignorance and apathy, and, under the shadow of British justice, live and thrive on the gains of injustice.

The Golden East! You have but to scratch the plating with the nail of your forefinger to find that it is a mere tinsel thing which disguises about as much real prosperity as the phrase "the good old days when George the Third was King!"

CHAPTER XII

ON THE PATH OF PROGRESS

"PAN is not dead in India. The Unchanging East abides, though not without betraying by the hem of its garments what ways it has been forced to walk in."

What ways are those? You may summarise them as the Path of Progress. The Unchanging East, after reclining for two thousand years on a civilisation established before Christ was born, has within the last three decades begun to stir on its couch, to look around it, to stretch out its foot, feeling the path.

The rude hand of the West has been laid on its shoulder and shaken it from its long sleep, and the historian of Hindustan must date the awakening of India from the second half of the Victorian era. Let us count a few of the milestones on this path which is just begun.

First and foremost is the Suez Canal. Then steam communication with the West, railways, telegraphs, a halfpenny post, irrigation, a fixed standard of silver, and education. These are the factors that are changing the Unchanging East.

The path has been rapidly made; the sleepers are aroused and bidden to walk upon it. Whither shall it lead them? Are they, who have only just awakened from this long sleep, fit to walk? Those who have ventured the first mile, do they walk sedately? Is the path of progress suited to the genius of the Unchanging East?

Quien sabe? Time alone can tell. Current opinion cannot focus current history. All we can do is to write the chronicle of change as it appears to us; to note facts and leave inferences to a future when their value may be better discriminated and judged. We are too near the stage where the transformation scene is being set.

Let us glance first at education, which has been brought within the reach of the great unread. In the opinion of some, it has not been an unmixed blessing. In general, it has turned the muddy end of the stick into the handle, and, in particular, has detached the ferrule from the performance of its proper functions.

The Indian aristocracy and gentry is a little apt, like the English peerage in a previous century, to consider itself above the vulgar necessity of education. One of the privileges of being rich is being ignorant. Moreover, under the system of education which has been introduced, a levelling tendency has crept in, which is foreign to the spirit of caste. In the Government schools there is a mingling of all ranks of society, and, as a fact, the trading castes, which are quite contemptible to the priestly and warrior ones, are most numerously represented. If in England reading and writing could only be acquired through the medium of board schools, they might not be such universal accomplishments amongst the aristocracy.

The Hindus are people of receptive intellect, and have a remarkable facility for assimilating knowledge. In addition, they are marvellously industrious and painstaking. They have learned that knowledge is power—the only power within their reach. In the scheme of their society, the Brahmins have ever been the brain-power, and, even in the days of Mahomedan ascendency, directed the administration. For centuries, they monopolised the higher education amongst men, as nautch-girls did amongst women. When schools and universities were introduced, the inferior castes were not slow to perceive the opportunity which education afforded of rising to dignity, power, and emolument undreamed of before. And although the subtle Brahmin brain still retains its ascendency, cunning commercial intelligence is fast shouldering it.

Thus education is beginning to sap at the very foundations of Hindu civilisation; it is appropriating the power which has hitherto been the monopoly of the priestly caste for the lower orders. The native has his son taught English with one sole aim in view—a Government appointment. There are, of course, other occupations to fall back upon, such as the law, a commercial clerkship, and so forth. But the come-down is as great as that of an Englishman who, having crammed for the Indian Civil, is compelled to accept an appointment in a bank, or find refuge in the overstocked ranks of the bar.

The Government appointments are few, and the applicants many, for the Indian universities turn out their wares by the thousand annually, and the schools by tens of thousands. The ware is often Brummagem, for whilst you can polish the Hindu intellect to a very high pitch, you cannot temper the Hindu character with those moral and manly qualities which are essential for the positions he seeks to fill. Moreover, the loaves and fishes fall far short of the multitude, and the result is the creation of armies of hungry "hopefuls"—the name is a literal translation of the vernacular generic term *omédwár* used in describing them—who pass their lives in absolute idleness, waiting on the skirts of chance, or gravitate to courses entirely opposed to those which education intended.

I have often talked the matter over with native friends in the district where I resided, in which was a high school where English was taught up to a fairly superior standard. It was well attended by the sons of small traders and well-to-do farmers, who formed as good material to draw deductions from as you could wish. The first thing to be noted from the education their boys received was that it rendered them absolutely unfitted for the occupations their fathers followed in a land where callings are hereditary; the second that it filled them with an overweening false pride, and taught them to despise their fathers.

"My sons are no good to me whatever," sighed my head-overseer to me constantly, who had sent his two boys to be educated, and never ceased regretting it. "They are too fine to put their hands to honest work as I have done these twenty years past. They will not even look after the farm at home, because they are 'educated.' They can get no employment through their education, and all they do is to swagger about the house like young rajahs, spend money, live in idleness, laugh at or abuse every one on the strength of their superior knowledge, and constantly disgrace themselves because they have no work to do to keep them out of mischief! I wish to God I had never sent them to school. But I had an idea they would both rise to be magistrates and judges." The same opinion, in substance, was repeated to me by many other fathers, and the local schoolboy came to be a byword for the effete, impudent, and useless. I have heard my coolie boys use their condition as a term of contempt: "He cannot prune any better than a schoolboy," they would say of a new hand, with a twinkle in their eyes as they glanced in the direction of the overseer.

Of these educated youths, at least ninety per cent. were choked off higher studies by the expense of the university, and left neither fish, flesh, fowl, nor good red herring, but useful subjects spoilt by the useless smattering of English which they had received. What of the other ten per cent.? A great percentage failed to pass their degrees, and returned to the ranks of the unemployed. The rest, having acquired the right to the letters B.A. after their names, joined the army of "hopefuls," and proceeded to squat down on their haunches and wait. But the call seldom came, and after a time they filtered into the legal profession, and battened on the native love for litigation, or became demagogues and aired their opinions in the native Press, which is often scurrilous and disloyal.

English education is the natural beginning of Europeanising. Very early in the day it takes the form of modifying the native costume, and the native discontinues shaving his head, adopts tailor-made garments, takes to wearing shoes and stockings, and only retains his turban as the link between him and the caste he has practically renounced. And now his soul begins to expand, and he apes the *sahib*. The transformation has a wondrous effect on his humbler brethren, who flatter and fawn on him, whereby his conceit rises like the mercury in hot weather. He adopts the "English air," and becomes bumptious; certain it is his manners are not improved, who mistakes a vulgar self-assertion for independence. And he looks on the wine when it is red. Such conduct, when the beverage is English brandy, is a parting from the ways of caste.

Having thus broken free from the shackles of his birth, he desires to distinguish himself in a sphere cognate to his new acquirements, and decides on making a start in *Nukkle Sluff*, which being interpreted means "Local Self-Government."

The principle of representative government has of recent years been started in India by the creation of municipalities and local and district boards, some of the seats on which are filled by election. The native is absolutely apathetic about them, and when he takes the trouble to vote is usually guided by the caste of the candidate. The Europeanised native, with his glib tongue, his superior education, his assurance, and his flattery, an art he has by no means forgotten, experiences no difficulty in getting elected. He now begins to practice the craft of oratory, and works on the minds of men. He is soon deep in jobbery and corruption, as the municipalities of Bombay and Calcutta have demonstrated. Every Indian *Nukkle Sluff* is a Tammany Hall on a small scale.

From this sphere the next step is to become a "Congress-*Wallah*," which is the height of his ambition. In the reign of Lord Ripon there was a departure in English policy, and the principles of liberalism were sought to be introduced into the conservatism of the Hindus. It awakened new aspirations in the breast of the native who was educated, and from those aspirations sprang a National Congress, or annual gathering of representatives from all parts of India, whose advertised aim was to "bring all men of light and leading together, to foster a public spirit, to educate the people, and familiarise them with the working of representative institutions, and to demonstrate to the British Government that India is ripe for self-government."

Theoretically a noble programme; but in practice it began by passing resolutions approving the abolition of the Council of the Secretary of State for India, recommended holding the Indian Civil Service examinations in India for half the appointments, the sanctioning of a native volunteer corps, and the repeal of the Arms Act. I need not quote more of a policy which, if adopted, would place arms in the hands of the natives to deluge the land in blood directly native administration and representative institutions brought Hindus and Mahomedans—ever ready to fly at each other's throats—in contact. And when these proposals are made by the spokesmen, self-elected, of effeminate races, who shudder at the sight of a drawn sword, they dwindle into a farce. Nor are they regarded as anything better than a farce in India, where the Mahomedans despise the Congress, the native nobility holds contemptuously aloof from it, the peasant does not even know of its existence, and the native Press derides it.

But the Congress-*Wallah* is blessed with brazen lungs and assurance, and able to make himself heard far and wide; he has a catchy cry, "India for the Indians," and it finds an echo in some quarters in England, where there are folk who take him seriously. Self-government in India is impossible; the country is too cosmopolitan, the racial hatreds too intense. But self-government under the Congress-*Wallah*, who represents the failures amongst those who set forth to win official employ, is a contingency too ludicrous to contemplate what time the fierce Mahomedans, the stalwart Sikhs, and the fighting Rajpoots—silent folks at present—shall begin to take an interest in the problem. And, after all, what is the so-called National Congress but a debating society, which represents the Empire as little as the Oxford Union Society represents the United Kingdom—nay, less; for whereas the Oxford undergraduate illustrates much that is best and most virile in our life, the Congress-*Wallah* merely represents himself, who is but a cheap stucco image operating on a wind-bag.

This digression has taken me rather further than I intended. The moral I would draw is that Western education grafted on Eastern character is an impossible combination. "The educated native," says Mr. Lilly, in his admirable book on the *Problems of India*, "is in no sense a representative of the great mass of the inhabitants of India, and has no sort of influence with them. The vast bulk of the population, the cultivators of the land, know and care nothing about him. The hardy warlike races, who furnish our best soldiers, utterly despise him. He is not, ordinarily, a product of whom our rule should be proud." And yet he is the foremost representative on the path of progress, and the man who aspires to take the reins from English hands. And he is what English education has made him: a poor thing—but their own!

There are those who believe that if ever another rebellion breaks out in India it will be at the instigation of the educated classes, and that the danger lies in the mischievous and disloyal propaganda of the Bengali Baboos and the Mahratta Brahmins. Should these predictions be fulfilled, the Congress-*Wallah* will have justified himself, for he prints and preaches veiled sedition. The question remains whether England shall have justified her system, which has created a breed of demagogues in a land of fanatical racial hatreds, and a host of "young hopefuls," who, in learning to speak English in broken periods, have grown too proud to earn their own bread in their hereditary callings.

It is a pleasant transition to the material progress of India. The expanding revenue is the best index to its commercial as distinct from its rural prosperity. The country has been seamed with a network of railways, so that you can now travel from Cape Comorin to Peshawur, or from Karachi to Assam, without changing carriages; it has been opened out with roads and bridges that have brought the farthest jungles into communication with the busy centres of life. For eightpence you can despatch a telegram two thousand miles, and the halfpenny post has been an institution any time within these past thirty years. The prices current of European markets are known in India within an hour of their being shouted on the Exchanges of the Continent, and people grumble if their correspondence with England takes a fortnight in its transit. The Government has reclaimed enormous tracts of waste land with the finest system of irrigation in the world, run canals through arid provinces, and battled with famine with an energy that has halved its horrors. The development of the industrial resources of the country has been equally remarkable. Bombay is a city of cotton mills, cotton presses, and ginning factories; the exports of grain from India exceed thirty million hundredweights; Calcutta sends out its shiploads of jute by the hundred from the magnificent mills erected to deal with the fibre. The tea, coffee, and indigo concerns number considerably over a thousand; with tea more than half a million acres are planted, producing a hundred and eighty million pounds, and representing twenty millions sterling invested, whilst coffee exports thirty-two million pounds, and indigo from India is still held to be the best dye in the world. Coal is one of the most promising industries, and there are very rich gold mines in the Madras presidency. Western civilisation, energy, and capital have developed all these and many other industries; have found markets for them, and, more important still, the means of getting the produce to the markets. Their establishment has created a revolution in the industrial life of India, which, although it possessed all these resources, was never able to utilise them until British rule brought peace to pursue the arts of peace, and enterprise to push them forward.

Nor can I pass over "fixity of exchange" without mention. India is a land of silver currency, for you never see a golden coin in circulation there. So long as silver retained its old relative value to gold, and the rupee could be exchanged for a florin, which it approximated in weight, there were no fiscal difficulties in the way of commerce. But as gold began to become "appreciated," and the discoveries of mountains of silver deteriorated the value of that metal, the Indian rupee dropped in value, till you could only exchange it for a shilling of English coinage, that was sustained by a gold reserve. The inherent speculations of commerce were doubled and tripled by the speculations of exchange, until Lord Elgin grasped the bull by the horns, and boldly fixed the rate at which the raw metal should be issued from the mints of India, irrespective of its intrinsic worth. By a stroke of the pen, a gold standard was established in a country of silver currency, and the rupee became a fixed instead of a fluctuating token. Had India been left to its own resources in the economical crisis that was brought about by the depreciation of silver, her currency would have been halved in value as a purchasing power in countries where the standard is a gold one, and she must have been shut off from many of the Western luxuries she now enjoys, whose prices would have been increased thirty-three per cent. in her own coinage, as compared to what they are to-day.

"*Si monumentum requiris, circumspice!*" What the English have accomplished in India must ever be the best monument of their right to be there. There are those who have cried, "Perish India!"—the best way to bring about that result would be to withdraw from ruling it. For the edifice they have reared, and are rearing, needs the eye and the genius of the architect to continue its building. The foundation is the Unchanging East, but the stones are carried from the West. There is no builder in the Orient who can take charge of the plan, which is assuredly the boldest experiment that the English, the only successful Empire-builders in the world of to-day, have ever attempted.

ANGLO-INDIAN LIFE

CHAPTER XIII

THE LAND OF EXILE

INDIA has often been called "The Land of Regrets." It is the logical result of exile. The pervading sentiment in Anglo-Indian life is the consciousness of exile; the dearest word and thought, "Home." And yet, curiously enough, there are few retired Anglo-Indians who are not often heard to wish themselves back in India!

I have never been able to decide in my mind whether the charms of Anglo-Indian life outbalanced its defects. It is such a mass of contradictions; of sunshine and gloom, of luxury and squalor, of comfort and discomfort. You recall one phase with delight to shrink at the reminiscence of another. India is something more than a foreign country, it is a fantastic country, and it is almost impossible to come at a comparison between the conditions there and those in England, because they differ as much as life at sea and on shore.

People in England have a habit of beginning all conversations with a reference to the weather; this can hardly be avoided when you come to talk of India, for the climatic conditions dominate life there, and make it for the greater part of the year an indoor one. Take a census of the European population any time between ten and four, from March to September, and you shall find it indoors. This, of course, is a very stale piece of information, and you may retort that all office-men and most women in England suffer the same confinement. True, but from a very different necessity, and under very different conditions. There are times on a hot summer's day when indoors becomes oppressive even in England: it is always oppressive in India. At seasons it is overpoweringly so, as when you live for two or three months at a stretch in a bath of perspiration, and wonder whether you will ever know what it is to be cool again. It debilitates and depresses; the punkah that sways above you with its drowsy rise and fall, and keeps you imprisoned to a square of the carpet, is either an irritant or a soporific; the darkened room affects you with the sadness of a perpetual twilight. Life resolves itself into a negative state, and inanition supervenes on apathy. There are six hundred minutes in some Indian hours, I am sure, and not one of them bearable.

The new arrival, in his fever of Saxon energy and impatience, puts on a hat (that is in itself a handicap on ordinary comfort) and makes a plunge into the roasting sunshine. If under such conditions you can train your mind to think of anything so delicious as an icy blast, it may be said that the east wind is tempered to the shorn lamb; for it is undoubtedly the case that the "Griffin"—who corresponds to the "New Chum" of the Colonies—feels or fears the heat much less than the presumably hardened old stager. I cannot explain this, but it is notorious, and the old Anglo-Indian who returns to England will often find its summer temperature more oppressive than a man who has never experienced a tropical one.

But when you have dared the sun, and are once out of doors in India, what do you gain by it? I vow the only thing more physically disagreeable than indoors is out of doors, and you must be very much in a hurry to see the country to stick to the exchange. There is nothing to recommend it, and your last state is worse than your first. There are only heat, glare, dust, thirst, perspiration, flies, and a conviction that you are not in your proper element; and that is what makes the imprisonment of indoor life in India so hard to suffer—there is absolutely no refuge from it.

Except for the members of the commercial community, India is a land of locomotion and unsettled habitation. Two or three years in any one "station," as towns are called, is the utmost that can be anticipated. No man lays himself out for a long residence any where, and a permanent home is an unknown quantity to the majority of Anglo-Indians, whose life is practically passed in a succession of furnished apartments. Far more often than not his furniture is hired, and his bungalow rented on a monthly tenancy, so that he may always be ready to strike his tents and shift station at the shortest notice. A man deems himself lucky who is permitted to pass four undisturbed years in one district.

It must not be presumed from my reference to furnished apartments that there are such conveniences in the East, except in the sense that house and furniture are both rented. In city life, a few men reside in hotels, which are cheaper in India than anywhere I know of in the world, the charge being seven to eight shillings a day, and the comfort in ratio to the charge. In the finest hotel in Bombay you will be supplied with only one knife, fork, and spoon, which will be taken away and cleaned after every course! In Calcutta there are a great number of boarding-houses, but the average Englishman, be he married or single, has to keep up his own house and establishment. With bachelors, "chumming" is very common, where there is any one to chum with, but, taken on the whole, life is solitary and ungregarious.

Locomotion is rendered comparatively easy by the railways, but the distances that have to be traversed are enormous. I remember once being a week in trains travelling from Calicut to Lahore, and two to three days is quite an ordinary journey. For shorter distances, every one who can manage it travels by night. No European travels third-class, and as many as can first, the charge for which is a fraction over a penny a mile. There are in every train carriages set aside for ladies, an arrangement which is very necessary when the railway carriage practically becomes a place of residence for two or three days. Every carriage is a saloon or half-saloon, with a bathroom and lavatory attached, and the seats are so constructed that the backs turn up and form couches or bunks. It is the universal practice in India to carry your bedding about with you; in fact, no one ever leaves home for a single night without his proper complement of quilts, sheets, and pillows, so that the matter of bed-clothes gives no trouble. Male passengers habitually undress and tumble into *pyjamas*, and ladies adopt the *negligé* of a dressing-gown. Meals are provided at "Refreshment-room stations" at stated intervals on the line, and, being ordered in advance by the guard, are always ready when the train draws up; the charges vary from two to three shillings for breakfast, tiffin (the Anglo-Indian name for luncheon), and dinner. In the hot weather, the guard always carries ice and soda-water in his van, and these can be purchased at any stopping station *en route*. A dining-car is unknown in India, where, judging by the length of stoppages at insignificant stations, saving time is of little consideration. The speed of the trains varies from sixteen to twenty-five miles an hour, with the exception of a few mail trains, which may attain thirty. This is quite in accord with the sentiment of the East, where hurry is against the etiquette of native good manners.

A great deal of travelling in India has to be accomplished by horse transit, and a *tonga*, which is a sort of two-horsed dog-cart, is the commonest vehicle in use, and ambles along at the rate of six miles an hour. After this comes the *dák-gharrie*, which runs on four wheels. In this you may bridge over the seats, spread your bedding out, and take your ease. Failing these methods of crossing country there is the *dhoolie-dák*, or palanquin, which still survives in some of the out-of-the-way places. Here you are carried in a recumbent position in a closed-in litter on the shoulders of four men, with a couple to relieve, at a stereotyped pace of three miles an hour, and in a cloud of dust churned up by their shuffling feet. The experienced *dhoolie-dák* traveller never allows his *dhoolie* to be set on the ground, whereby he avoids exasperating detentions at the stages where the bearers are changed. In these methods of travelling you put up at *dák-bungalows*, or Government hostelries, which are erected all along the main Indian roads. They are comfortless places as a rule, in charge of a cook who generally catches and kills a fowl for you when you arrive, and serves it up within twenty minutes. The *dák-bungalow* is one of the trials of Anglo-Indian life, and has probably had more jokes fathered upon it than English seaside lodging houses; but when you are in one, the joke is not appreciable.

Such are the means by which the *Moffussil*, "up-country," or provincial Anglo-Indian will reach his station or district, and unless he is going to Bombay or Calcutta, which are practically the two entrance doors of the Empire, with Madras for a back door, his first experience of Anglo-Indian life will be of travel; and the land journey will often prove much more trying than the sea-voyage. India is, as I have called it, a Land of Locomotion.

Outside the principal cities and towns of India, shopping is impossible. This does not refer to household shopping, which is always left to the servants, for, wherever you are, it is beneath your dignity to have personal transactions with your butcher, baker, grocer, or milkman. But European luxuries, which include wines and tinned provisions, you may select yourself without any loss of caste. India luxuriates in hermetically sealed stores: tinned salmon and lobster, tinned bacon and cheese, tinned soups and sausages, tinned asparagus and fruit, tinned jam and potted meats—good heavens! what is there that is not tinned? These are the dainties of Anglo-Indian daily life, the delicacies of the dinner-party. "I suppose," the "country-bred" belle is reported to have said, "the Queen of England has tinned tid-bits at every meal!" They correspond with the truffles and turtle-soup of English banquets. I remember a very worthy Scotchman who used to allow himself a tinned Finnan haddock every Sunday for breakfast; he said it was an extravagance, but it reminded him of Scotland! I have myself found tinned lobster in the solitudes of the Himalayas reminiscent of the Isle of Sark, where I spent the most delightful holiday of my life. Taste is as great a refresher of memory as smell.

In small up-country stations there are generally one or two "Europe shops," kept more often than not by Parsees, where one can purchase the most miscellaneous assortment of articles, ranging from patent medicines and Scotch whisky to composite candles and Christmas cards. But for other tradesmen, such as the tailor, bootmaker, draper, and barber, you send for them to attend you. Your tailor, indeed, you often keep on the premises, for the Indian *derzie*, or knight of the needle, squats in the verandah, and can adapt his art to either sex, turning out hot-weather suits of white drill, or tea-gowns, or summer frocks with a sort of ambidexterity. The hat is another affair; in the land of the turban you will do well not to rely on the vernacular hatter. It is well to obtain your *topee* from a reliable source, for the native-made head-gear of the *Moffussil*, a monstrous "mushroom" made out of pith an inch in thickness, is the sort of thing to provide novelty and amusement in a pantomime. Your washerman is your private property, and resides on the premises; if you are a bachelor, you pay him four or five shillings a month, and he does all your washing; even if it runs to seven suits of white drill clothes and fourteen shirts a week there is no extra charge. The Anglo-Indian changes his linen very frequently, and when he returns to England the first thing he curses is the laundry bill.

Beyond the necessaries of life, whatever you want you must send for by post. There is a system in India called the "Value Payable Post," or briefly "V.P.P.," by which the value of the parcel delivered is at time of delivery recovered from the purchaser, who must pay before he gets his goods. This has been a great boon to the shopkeepers of the country, where, until its institution, credit was universal, and not always immaculate. All petty shopping is done by V.P.P.; it is the recognised arrangement, and seldom abused except where the unkind cut is practised of sending an old unpaid bill, receipted, through its medium. The European tradesmen of the cities make this method of shopping easy by distributing the most elaborate illustrated catalogues and price-lists, many of them in bulk equal to the *Field*. The nuisance of circulars is greater in Anglo-India than in England.

One of the luxuries of England is the daily morning paper to be purchased everywhere and in endless variety. Except on the line of rail in India, you cannot buy a paper, and then only for fourpence in the majority of cases, though a penny paper exists in Calcutta. The *Pioneer*, or *Englishman*, or *Times of India* is always received by post, and imparts a peculiar sense of welcome to the man in scarlet, the distinctive uniform of the Indian postman. The craving for home news is very marked, and the London cablegrams are the first things glanced at or inquired about. They not unfrequently constitute the one excitement of the Indian day. After them, the advertisement columns attract as much attention as any other, for here you shall glean much personal information that is vastly interesting. You do your shopping from them as a matter of course, but more edifying than this is to learn who is selling-off and going home. For the first thing an Anglo-Indian does who premeditates a trip to England is to advertise his household goods in the Press. If you want to buy a piano, horse, dog, tent, dinner service, or anything substantial in value, your first course is to scan the advertisement columns of your paper, wherein from March to June, the season when every one desires to leave India, you can rely on a plethora of bargains offered to you; but prices go up from October to December, when all who are on leave, and can fix their own time, return to the country, and are "on the buy."

The Indian daily paper is far more to the Anglo-Indian than you would suppose; it is his living link with England, and its meagre cablegrams—for they are miserly meagre—bring delight to thousands of exiles. That feeling of being "in touch with home" cannot be understood by any one who has not left it. There are men parted from those they hold most dear who keep account of the approximate speed of the various mail steamers, and will tell you at a moment's notice whether the week's mail may be expected a day earlier or a day later than the average, or on the contract date. And they eagerly trace its course from Brindisi to Port Saïd, from Port Saïd to Aden, from Aden to Bombay, and are all agog to know whether a special train has been put on to expediate the bags to their part of India. That is where the sense of exile comes in,—the looking and longing for the English mail.

Except in the Hills, which are elevated sanatoriums on the slopes of the Himalayas or other mountain ranges, and which correspond to English holiday resorts, there is not much walking done in India. First of all the act of walking is derogatory, and no native gentleman ever travels on "Shanks' mare." When a viceroy indulged in a walking tour in the Himalayas the natives were scandalised. Then, again, the majority of Europeans keep at least one horse and trap. You may almost call it a necessity for the European character. In the commercial centres an "office carriage" is often kept for the clerks of the mercantile houses, or at least a palanquin. At those times when the English would consider walking a pastime the Anglo-Indian rides or drives; a gentle stroll in the cool of the evening is the limit of his exertions, except when he is out shooting. Of course, climate has a good deal to do with this lassitude, not to say laziness; but when people can afford horse-flesh, it is extraordinary how soon they learn to become "carriage-folk," who had never kept a carriage in England did they live there for a century. The cost of keeping a horse is comparatively small, though each horse has a groom and grass-cutter attached to it; you may put it down at about fifteen-pence a day, and the purchase of a hack at twenty pounds, though a "country-bred" can be picked up much cheaper.

Drinking is far more prevalent in Anglo-India than in England. Up-country, to omit offering a "peg," which almost invariably assumes the form of a whisky and soda, is a great lapse from propriety and decency. But the Indian "peg," albeit copious, is fairly innocuous, a small modicum of spirit being usually drowned in a pint of aerated water. Many men fight shy of beer on account of liver; light wines are coming more into favour; but brandy, once the typical Anglo-Indian drink, is unknown. Of course, the thirst is abnormal, and a long drink before midday probably the custom. But by eleven o'clock, when the sun is supposed to come over the fore-arm, the Anglo-Indian has been up for five or six hours, and for my part I always considered that the middle of the working-day, and a legitimate hour to refresh. The really insidious time for "pegging" is in the cool hours of the evening after sunset, and before dinner, when people meet for company and too often for conviviality. But, taking him for all in all, the Anglo-Indian has made a greater stride towards sobriety in the last thirty years than England did in the nineteenth century, which is saying a good deal. Without calling him temperate, I should decidedly call him a sufficiently sober soul, considering the aggravating conditions of thirst under which he lives.

The food in India, whilst far inferior in the raw material to that of England, is rendered much more tasty by the excellence of the cooking. No one ever sits down to a dinner of less than four courses, and the native *chef* is peculiarly skilful at *entrées*, or "side dishes," as they are called. The country itself provides some excellent appetisers, and *pillaos*, *ketcheries*, and curries will tempt the most jaded palate when English cooking would nauseate it. For tiffin in the hottest weather there is nothing like currie. Joints are at a discount in a country where all the meat is bad, and people who turn up their noses at Australian mutton would find it convenient to be born snub-nosed for a residence in the East. Chicken is the standard dish of India, and beef the least consumed. Eggs enter very largely into the dietary, but they are small, scarce bigger than bantams'; and, in the season, game can be shot or purchased almost everywhere.

There is no difficulty in making acquaintances in India, for the first call is the prerogative of the last arrival. Every Anglo-Indian's bungalow stands in its own garden, and at the gate hangs suspended a board with his name painted on it. Each station is a directory in itself, and all the new-comer requires is a sheaf of visiting-cards. Having delivered these he enters society, and his subsequent experience depends upon himself. Hospitality, though behind the standard of the pre-Suez-Canal days, is still a shining virtue of the Anglo-Indian, and a stranger who is able to make himself agreeable is never a stranger long. His chief difficulty will be to avoid the cliques into which society in the East habitually falls; this is perhaps a natural result in a community where every one knows every one, and a splitting up into groups of affinities is the corollary,—and not only knows every one else, but his income, his prospects, and his particular social status in a select population governed by the strictest laws of precedence. There have been more quarrels over precedence in Anglo-India than over any other cause; it is regulated by a table edited and issued by Government, which is, in effect, the charter of Anglo-Indian society. Ladies are pedantically jealous, and woe betide the unhappy hostess who makes some quite unintentional error in the order in which she sends her guests in to dinner. It often leads to a row royal. When it becomes very acute, some one pitches the Table of Precedence at the parties, as Moses did the Tables of the Law, and that settles it.

And talking of Anglo-Indian ladies, their position in the East is not what it was. The fatal Canal supplied them in such legions that the difficulty of the modern hostess is to get dancing men, not spinsters. In the "good old days," a ball was often put off when it was known that an unmarried girl or two—"spins," as they are called in Anglo-Indian phrase—were *dáking* up to the station, consequent on the arrival of a ship from England; nowadays it is deferred until a polo match of *gymkhana* (a gathering for sports) is due, to bring the men into headquarters. When I went out to India in 1871, there were nine "spins" in a passenger-list of forty, and all were married within the year; returning in 1896 in a P. and O. mail steamer, there were more blighted ambitions on board than I counted. The modern Anglo-Indian is prone to marriage, but he goes home to get him a wife in the majority of cases. And if there is one thing he avoids, it is the "country-bred."

"Country" is a peculiar adjective in Anglo-Indianism that at once diminishes the value of anything. It is a sneer and a condemnation. A "country-bred" individual is at once stigmatised by the appellation. "Country-made" goods are a synonym for inferiority. On the other hand, anything "English" or "imported" at once acquires a special value, and an imported dog, iron bedstead, carpet, or article of furniture stamps the owner as a man of taste and means, and sheds dignity over him. "What is she?" a man asks, nodding towards a pretty brunette in a ballroom. "Oh, only a C. B." That suffices. But you must know your audience in using the initials. There is a story told of a gentleman who was extolling the merits of a certain handsome young official, already a Companion of the Bath, to a lady of the country, and observed he was a "C. B." "What is that?" she inquired, half daring, half doubting, for she could not believe the individual in question was not "imported." "A Companion of the Bath," came the explanation. "Oh, you must not speak to me like that!" was the protest of the coy creature.

CHAPTER XIV

ANGLO-INDIAN CASTES

YOU can divide Anglo-Indian society into castes as precisely as you can the Hindus. The Civil Service, or administrative class, represents the Brahmins, with their privileges, their power, and their precedence of all others. In the military, you have an exact counterpart of the warrior caste, and, in its relation to the Brahmins, identical. The mercantile element represents the trading castes, and the "British workman" on railways and in mills, shops, and offices is a *Vaishya*, or of the labouring caste; whilst to complete the parallel, the Eurasian, or half-caste, is the pariah of Anglo-Indian society. Unconsciously, but exactly, these groups represent those in the Hindu scale in their opinions of themselves and their relations to one another.

The English Brahmins are divided into as many sections as their native prototypes. First comes the "I.C.S.-*Wallah*," or Indian Covenanted Civilian, who is the salt of the earth, a Benares Brahmin, so to speak, with the umbrella of importance always over him. There are about a thousand civilians entitled to put those magic initials, which stand for "Indian Civil Service," after their names; all the other civilians are "Uncovenanted Civilians," which is quite another pair of shoes. But, be they covenanted or uncovenanted, they monopolise all the best-buttered pieces of bread in the Indian Empire.

The Indian Civil Service is the highest paid of any in the world, and offers more plums of appointment, with a salary always munificent, a pension of a thousand a year after twenty-one years' service, and, in the event of death, four hundred a year to the widow and a hundred and fifty to each of his daughters. From the ranks of this privileged class, a man may rise to be the Lieutenant of a Province as large as the United Kingdom, to several lesser spheres of ruling power and dignity, may become a State Secretary, a member of Council, or adorn several other posts, the emoluments of which vary from three to seven thousand pounds a year. And throughout his career, he is always favoured of what Mr. Kipling has called the "little tin gods," and carries his chin at a higher cock than any one else in Anglo-India.

The Covenanted Civilian has his weaknesses; for instance, he always inscribes the initials I.C.S. on his visiting-cards after his name, and on the board at the gate of his garden. This is to inform the world that he belongs to that higher Brahminism which looks coldly down on the rest. He is the aristocrat of a community which does not number more than one hundred and fifty thousand Britons, and represents the exclusiveness of the upper ten thousand in England. He is charged by his less fortunate fellow-creatures with being conceited and purse-proud; but this is probably due to jealousy in most instances. There is a covenanted civilian at the head of every district in India, who is a little king in his way, and rules society. He is expected to entertain and lead the fashion, and much depends upon the character of the individual and his wife. The service is recruited by competitive examination open to all, and brains, or to speak more correctly, cramming, wins its way to the front. Gentle birth is no longer an essential for employ in the service of the Indian Government, and you may, and sometimes do, find a tradesman's son in the ranks of the select service. In the old days of John Company, when appointments were given to nominees of the directors, the latter were sponsors for the social status of their candidate; but that is all changed under the present system, and perhaps not for the better.

Notwithstanding, and taking it all round, the administrators of the Indian Civil Service are probably as good as any in the Empire, and the foibles they display are no greater than you will find in England amongst members of Parliament and civic magnates. The civilian moults his feathers when he gets west of the Suez Canal, and sometimes becomes a very sparrow. I have seldom experienced such a shock as that of meeting on the top of a penny 'bus a "Commissioner," who had been the virtual ruler of four of the largest districts in Upper India, and who, when I had last seen him, was driving in a feudatory rajah's carriage, escorted by *sowars*, and through a city the population of which was in a state of ground-level prostration. "Look on this picture and on that," was my mental reflection, as I remembered the pomp and circumstance of his "receptions" in the East, when he never condescended to advance from a particular square of the carpet to greet his guests. But I cannot candidly say he was typical of any but a small class amongst his fellows who carry the rights of the divinity that doth hedge them to an absurd excess at times.

The lesser civilians in India,—the engineer, the doctor, the superintendent of police, and so forth—have each a dignity above the common, which is conferred by being in service under Government. This is, perhaps, natural in a country where nearly all the members of society, outside a few large cities, are in "the service," and their status laid down in those Tables of Precedence I have quoted, which take no account whatever of the non-official. How should it, since they are not concerned with him? But for him the fact remains, that in going to India to fulfil his destiny, and help to develop the land, he surrenders all claims to his own proper social rank in a bureaucracy that has no admittance for "outsiders."

The military caste comes next in the Anglo-Indian social scale, a position it does not altogether appreciate. Between civilians and military there has been an antipathy from the beginning, is now, and ever will continue to be. Even in India the soldier is a poor man, and few of the loaves and fishes fall to his share. It is difficult for him on his "hundreds" to compete with the civilian, whose income is reckoned by thousands, and the return of hospitality is a heavy tax on him. If it were not for the military mess system, the problem would be harder, for Anglo-Indian society is prodigal of entertainment. As it is, mess entertainments are proverbially the best of all, and there is no place for enjoying life so gaily and brightly as a military cantonment in the cold weather. And where you find the soldier there is the best polo, the best cricket, the best racing, the best *gymkhanas*, the best of every form of sport and pastime. Moreover, there is an absence of stiffness in military entertainments that contrasts pleasantly with the more elaborate profusion but rather "slow" hospitality of the civilian.

As I have said, there is no love lost, as classes, between the civil and military folk. They are different castes, and they keep to their own as distinctly as do the Brahmins and rajpoots. Between the individual members there is often a keen jealousy. The precedence nearly always belongs to the civilian, who, if he is head of the district, is the senior of the officer commanding. Not unfrequently tiffs occur amongst the exalted, and then society at once divides itself, and you have your civil and your military cliques, which are as oil and vinegar. Perhaps, on the whole, the soldier has the best of it, because his society is larger, and leaves him more independent, whilst the civilian has only half a dozen of his caste to gather round him.

There is a queer compound to be found in some of the provinces of India, known as the military civilian. He is a soldier in what is called "civil employ," and whilst retaining his military rank, is to all intents and purposes, except pay, and the privilege of the initials, an Indian civilian. There are military revenue officers, military magistrates, and even military judges, whose functions are purely peaceful. I have seen a district judge, who held the rank of a major in the army, trying a case with a cheroot in his mouth, and giving ear to the subtlest arguments of counsel; and a colonel addressing himself to the task of collecting revenue with nothing more threatening than a pen in his hand. One I remember whose boast it was that he had not put on a uniform for twenty years. The military civilian inclines to the manners and customs of the Brahmin rather than to those of the warrior caste, and in his habitual mufti seems to have sloughed off the military habit, and become a man of peace and plenty.

Descending from the Brahmin and warrior castes in Anglo-Indian society, it is a considerable step down to the trading caste. Into this classification fall merchants, planters, missionaries, manufacturers, barristers, and all those callings where the labour is not with the hands, but excluding shopkeepers, who are a caste to themselves. The custom of the East places these non-officials in the nondescript position of having no recognised social status by law prescribed. India is a land despotically governed, and the laws that govern its society are equally despotic. Nothing can be more humiliating than the status of the isolated non-official in an up-country station, where all the European community is composed of civilians or military officers. In the large mercantile centres, like Calcutta and Bombay, the non-official has his own society, and keeps to it; so, also, in the planting centres. But between these classes and the official ones there is decidedly a gulf fixed, and the civilian especially looks down on the trader who, for his part, eyes the official with something akin to amused contempt when exposed to his superciliousness.

But where the non-official is otherwise situated, he is very helpless. There is no such thing as public opinion in India outside the metropolitan cities, and the non-official has no voice in any matter. The Press of India does not represent public opinion, but the views of Government; its chief subscribers are Government officials, and it is dependent on the powers that be for news, not to mention fat contracts for advertising and printing. The non-official is without a vote, without representation, without privileges, and without rights, even though he be a free-born Englishman. He sacrifices all those when he enters on an Eastern career. In out-of-the-way places, he feels almost as if he were living on sufferance, and a man may be employing hundreds of labourers in a mill, or opening up thousands of acres of land that was waste, or introducing an industry that brings plenty to an impoverished district, and yet find himself considered socially of less account than the last young prig of an official out from Colville Gardens.

This social status is a little hard on the men who are the backbone of the prosperity of the country. The merchant, the manufacturer, and the planter are the people who have developed India, and brought Anglo-Saxon energy, not to mention capital, to work on its resources. The official may collect the revenue, but without the non-official, it would not have been one half of what it is at the present day. Moreover, there is a great jealousy of the non-official when he succeeds, and especially of that independence which the members of a bureaucratical form of government dare not display.

But harder than the lot of the English non-official gentleman in India is that of the Anglo-Saxon *Sudra*, as I may call the working-man.

He is an individual who labours with his hands in a country where all manual labour is far more derogatory than in England. You may say that no one need be ashamed of honest work, but where the white skin carries a racial superiority with it, the spectacle of one of the ruling race toiling with his hands before the natives is not edifying. It is necessary, but it is anomalous. When one boards the homeward-bound steamer there is always a sense of the unfit in being waited upon by the English stewards. This is work you are accustomed to associate with native menials only, and it takes you some time to pick up again those little amenities in accepting service which you have never vouchsafed your *bearer* or *kitmudghar*.

Tommy Atkins is redeemed by his uniform, which carries honour and *éclat* with it, but the grimy ganger on the railway, the European constable in the larger cities, and, worst of all, the English coachman employed by some of the wealthier natives, and the ladies'-maids whom certain ladies think it fashionable to keep, jar mightily against sentiment in a land where all manual and menial service is done by natives. At the same time, I am bound to admit that the British working-man is well able to "keep his end up," and even though he be a "poor white" in a population where most whites are tolerably well off, he asserts the birthright of his white skin not without energy. But I must say for my own part that, for choice, I should prefer the equal conditions of England at a lower wage to the social surrender every one must yield who takes pick and shovel in hand in the East. You cannot get away from caste in India, and that is against caste.

The pariah, or outcaste of Anglo-Indian society is found in the Eurasian, descended from a white father and a native mother, and the intermarriage of their offspring. There are as many Eurasians in India as there are pure whites, and they carry all shades of complexion, from one so fair that you cannot distinguish it from a European's to shades considerably darker than many of the native races.

In America, a half-caste who has less than half white blood in his veins is described as a quadroon or octoroon; the Anglo-Indian system is even more definite. The assessment follows the coinage. Thus the phrase "He is eight, six, four, or two annas in the rupee" (as the case may be) describes the Eurasian with analytical accuracy. "Eight annas," or half a rupee, designates the actual half caste; "four annas" those of one white and one half-caste parent, and six and two annas the intermediate degrees. It is all calculated to a nicety by this mathematical method. The prejudice against black blood is insuperable, and the merest "touch of the tar-brush" is sufficient to create a stigma. The Eurasian speaks with a peculiar accent, called *chi-chi*, which is considered very objectionable; he makes his final "y's" into "e's," and is in difficulty with his "th's." For instance, he would render "D'Arcy

Macarthy come to the city," "Darcee Macartee com to dee citee." The Anglo-Indian ear is very sharp to recognise *chi-chi bât.*

The Eurasian occupies an unenviable position. He is too proud to mix with the natives, who will, indeed, have none of him, and the European shuns him. He is a sort of social neutral stratum, regarded as foreign and looked upon with suspicion by the brown race, and looked down on with contempt by the white. Popularly supposed to inherit all the vices and none of the virtues of his parents, there is little ever said in his favour. I fear you cannot call the Eurasian trustworthy or truthful as a class, though of course there are many honourable exceptions. Certain it is he seldom rises to high employ, and is chiefly engaged in clerkly duties, for he has an unconquerable aversion to physical work or energy of any sort. The Eurasian society is one apart and unique, and its etiquette and manners are often a fine burlesque on those of the white race, with which its members are proud to claim connection. Their womenfolk affect gaudy colours, and a Eurasian ball will display as many rainbow tints as a mulatto one. Some of the Eurasian girls are very beautiful when young, and not a few Europeans have succumbed to their charms, and married them; but such alliances are regarded with extreme disfavour when they occur among the higher grades of official life. As for the lower-class Eurasian men, it would be difficult to tell them from natives except for their European costume, and the fact that they do not shave their heads and do part their hair. The Portuguese have left behind a monument of their Indian dominion in a very numerous race of half-breeds, who hail from Goa. They enter largely into domestic service, and in Bombay all the best cooks and waiters are of Portuguese extraction. Nor will you find, in the whole of India, any better servants than these, with their white Eton jacket, collar and shirt, and bare feet. In this latter point they have adopted the custom of the natives without discarding that of the European, and the Goa boy comes into your presence without hat or shoes.

Of all the minor problems in India, "What shall we do with the Eurasians?" is perhaps the most difficult. They have just cause for complaint in the treatment they receive from the European, whose attitude towards them is similar to that of the native towards the outcaste. And yet the European race is responsible for these despised folk, and they cling to their connection with the ruling class with a pride and persistency that is almost pathetic.

I have not mentioned the "loafer," which is the Anglo-Indian word for the European beggar. He exists. Volubility is his forte, and he is always *en route* to a distant district to take up an appointment. He generally keeps to the cities, but sometimes he "tours the provinces." He is a creditor on your bounty, and I do not know any man more difficult to get rid of. It is a sorry spectacle to see him tramping the highway, but he is a dangerous individual to give money to, for it is nearly always sure to go at the next native dram-shop. In ninety-nine cases out of a hundred, drink has brought him to his miserable condition. And yet he belongs to the ruling race, and as he tramps the road you will find every native giving him the right of it!

For it is the custom of the country for the black to bow before the white, and this continual surrender has its effect upon the dominant race. It is not a wholesome atmosphere for it. The aristocracy of colour has its evils; it engenders a false pride, a sense of superiority, an inflatedness of self, which is, perhaps, the weakest point in the Anglo-Indian's character. It does the average Anglo-Indian good to go to a colony, and live in a state of equality for a time; for he gets a little too overbearing in India, surrounded as he is by servility and constant fawning. The black background brings the white skin into extreme relief; the effect is too dazzling—on the white. Nothing does him more good than to go home to England, and be kept waiting by the young lady attendant at a post-office for a penny stamp, while she finishes her flirtation with the *Sudra*—or, as I should say, the shop assistant from next door!

CHAPTER XV

BUNGALOW LIFE

THE Anglo-Indian's bungalow is as different from an English house in its external appearance and internal arrangement as is a temple from a church. It is always a detached building standing in ground of its own, which is called the "compound," single-storied, rambling, and flat-roofed. The doors are ill-fitting and clumsy, the windows small and often not made to be opened, and a "sash" window is unknown. The walls are whitewashed or distempered, and the floors are of cement. Every room has direct access to a verandah, and all enter one into another, for there are no passages. Each bedroom has its own bath and retiring room, there being no drains in India. A room with a single door in it is unknown; all have two, and many three, four, and even six, and those leading into the verandahs are generally glazed, which saves windows. Very few bungalows have halls, the verandah in the front of the house doing duty for such. Cellarage does not exist, and naturally there are no fireplaces, save in those districts in the north of India where the nights are chilly in the "cold weather," which is the Indian name for winter. Except in the capital cities, water and gas are conspicuous by their absence, and you may call at every house between Cape Comorin and Cashmere without finding a bell to pull.

The kitchen is a detached building erected as far away as possible from the bungalow. The only connection with your commissariat allowed in the dwelling is the storeroom, invariably known in India as the "godown"; and the sole domestic duty of the diligent Anglo-Indian housewife is to "do her godown" every morning. The cook comes with an assortment of plates and pots, makes his suggestions for the *menus* of the day's meals, and proceeds to help himself to the exact amount of ingredients necessary for them. This is a check upon pilfering, for all Indian servants feed themselves, and at your expense if they can. Meat in its uncooked state is never kept in the house, and only brought there for casual inspection; and on the fowl that enters so largely into Anglo-Indian dietary you cast a discriminating eye as it is being chevied round the compound preliminary to slaughter. In the kitchen, the cooking arrangements are primitive. The "range" consists of half a dozen small open fireplaces, each about eight inches square, grouped in a nest on the floor, or on raised masonry, and the fuel is wood or charcoal. Natives are so accustomed to the floor that they prefer to work on it; and a cook stirring a saucepan, is much more comfortable squatting on his haunches, than in a more elevated position.

The servants' "lines" are a row of huts, often mere hovels, adjoining the stables, and in the most distant corner of the compound. Each servant has one room, wherein dwell himself, wife, and family. If he is a Mahomedan he will not unfrequently enclose a small patch in front of his compartment with an erection of bamboo matting to form a screen, and thus secure the privacy of his *hareem*. The servants form a small colony in the compound, and a very moderate householder may find he is in practice the supporter of twenty human beings.

Very few ladies ever enter their kitchens. In the words of the poet, "'t is better not," for where ignorance is bliss, why set yourself against your food? But once a month, the prudent housewife inspects her cooking-pots, the reason being that they are always made of copper, and have to be periodically tinned, or they become poisonous. Many lives have been lost in India by the neglect of this precaution, and any sudden and inexplicable indisposition always elicits the question, "When were the *dekjies* last tinned?"

A bachelor's bungalow is not unfrequently a barn in appearance, for, with the constant shifting of residence, furnishing is reduced to a minimum. His goods and chattels are hired, and of the most primitive description. Anything uglier and more cumbersome than the Anglo-Indian's furniture it would be hard to find. All the chairs are cane-bottomed, heavy, and with arms, and the only comfortable ones are those for lounging in on the verandah, which have extending arms on which to elevate your legs. The tables are solid and ugly, generally a huge round one in the centre of the room and several small ones called "tea-poys," set indiscriminately about. A mat on the floor may or may not be relieved with a few rugs; but often the plaster is in bad repair, and crumbles under the foot. There are no blinds, and the curtains are purely practical, and not ornamental. If possible, the bedroom furniture is a cut more simple than that in the dwelling-rooms. A bed made of broad tape woven across a wooden framework is the usual couch for reposing on; a chest of drawers is a luxury, its place being more often taken by an *almirah*, or cupboard, with shelves in it. Looking-glasses have a way of distorting the visage which is useful in putting people out of conceit with themselves, but leads to bloodshed in shaving, unless, as is often the case, you turn your cheek to the barber, who gladly calls every morning. The toilette table is never draped, and the whole scheme of comfort is crude. All ablutions are performed in the bath-room, wherein a huge tub or zinc bath, and several clay *gurrahs* or earthen pipkins filled with water are the prominent features. Every one in India bathes once a day, and in the hotter districts often twice or thrice, with a night-bath thrown in. The bedding nearly always shows sign of travel, and has not that neat inviting appearance associated with the white counterpaned cot in England.

Notwithstanding the bare and desolate nature of the bachelor's abode, the Anglo-Indian lady generally manages to make the drawing-room in her bungalow pretty and artistic. There is great emulation in its decoration, and it surprises one to see what marvels of transformation can be effected by feminine taste and ingenuity. The first thing to catch the eye is the array of photographs displayed; it is the link with home. Then the tall ugly walls are hidden from sight with curtains, screens, fans, ornaments, and *phulkarries*. The floor is carpeted with a *dhurrie*, and the disposal of the furniture reflects resource if it sometimes leaves little space; whilst the piano at once brings you face to face with Western civilisation. It is generally iron-framed, and constructed to withstand the climate, before the scorching heat of which an English instrument acquires a habit of collapsing. The room is always dark, partly because there are no windows, but also for the sake of coolness, or imaginary coolness, the subdued light lending itself to that state of self-deception. All light has to filter into the rooms through the verandahs, and these are protected with "chicks," which are screens made of loosely woven slips of bamboo. They stretch from pillar to pillar, and in practice make rooms out of the verandahs. The doors are also guarded by similar contrivances to keep out flies. The trouble of drawing aside the chick on entering or leaving a room is one of the petty irritations of Indian life.

In her drawing-room, for the chief portion of the day, the Anglo-Indian lady is as much a prisoner by reason of the heat as the *zenana* woman is from custom. There is no shopping, and only the minimum of domestic duties to occupy her. She is by herself all day long, and thrown on her own resources of music, reading, letter-writing, or sketching. "The long, long, weary day" of the German song has been well parodied in one that bewails the "long, long, Indian day." The only break is when an afternoon caller drops in; but callers are few in an up-country station. And, besides, every one meets every one else at the universal gathering-place in the evening, which is probably the public gardens, "the Company's Garden," as it is still sometimes called in old-time association with the East India Company.

An afternoon nap is almost universal, if the flies will allow it. Flies by day and mosquitos by night are distinct trials. Most beds are smothered with mosquito curtains, which effectually keep away any little breath of air there is. But in the hotter districts no one ever dreams of sleeping without a punkah going all night, which is as necessary for rest and comfort as a pillow. The punkah, it is hardly needful to observe, is a huge swinging fan, pulled by a coolie, who squats in the verandah outside, and under it a great majority of Anglo-Indians pass their lives for no inconsiderable time of the year.

The servants in an Indian bungalow are numerous, though you have to engage many more in some presidencies than in others. In an average district, the bachelor will keep a cook, a man to do the waiting and house-work, a water-carrier, a horse-keeper, and probably a grass-cutter, a couple of punkah-coolies, and a scavenger, who is known as the "sweeper," and is an absolutely indispensable individual under the sanitary conditions that exist. A married man, living "comfortably," will be called on to keep a cook, table-attendant, bearer, who combines the duties of valet and housemaid, water-carrier, washerman, a couple of horse-keepers, and as many grass-cutters, ditto punkah-coolies, a gardener to keep the compound under cultivation, a *chupprassi* or *peon*, to hang about and make himself generally useful for messages and carrying letters, and a sweeper. In more extravagant households, the cook has his "mate" or scullion, and the number of table-attendants, bearers, and *chupprassis* is multiplied, as also the horse-keepers and gardeners; and in nearly every establishment there is a *derzie*, or tailor and milliner combined, who does all the mending. I have quite forgotten to mention the *ayah*, or lady's-maid, who is absolutely essential when there is a lady in the house. The cost of these establishments of servants will vary from three to twenty pounds and more a month, their wages ranging from six shillings for the punkah-coolies and grass-cutters to two pounds for the cook. It is a false economy to have a bad cook, for you want an artist to deal with the inferior raw material of the East, and to tempt the jaded appetite.

Rent is an expensive item. In a small up-country station you may get a bungalow for three pounds a month — salaries, wages, house-rent, bills, and everything in India, are, or should be, paid monthly—but five to ten pounds is the average rental, and in the metropolitan cities the cost is enormous, and people pay up to three and four hundred a year. Servants and house-rent are the two heaviest items in keeping up an Indian bungalow. Otherwise the cost of living is comparatively small. Bachelors very often contract with their cooks to feed them, paying a lump sum per month of from two to five pounds, and receiving in return breakfast, tiffin, and dinner, and early morning and afternoon tea. A lady who looks after her "godown" can do it for considerably less per head. In Bombay or Calcutta, most of the hotels and boarding-houses will lodge and feed a bachelor exceedingly well for ten pounds a month, and this saves all expense of servants except bearer and horse-keeper. When I first started housekeeping in the jungle, I used to pay two pounds for servant's wages, two pounds for house-rent, two pounds for my cook's contract for food, one pound for the keep of a horse, and allow three pounds for such luxuries as tinned English stores and liquors, lamp-oil, and the daily paper, which, in those days, meant eight shillings a month. And I lived like a fighting cock! A quarter of a century later, my household expenditure, including a considerably larger staff of servants, ranged from twenty to twenty-five pounds a month, and this is probably the average expended by the ordinary Anglo-Indian outside the centres where living is proverbially expensive. For myself, I did not notice much difference in the cost during those twenty-five years, and European luxuries were decidedly much cheaper and better. Meat varies from twopence to threepence a pound; bread is a penny a small loaf; vegetables, butter, and milk, the latter sold by weight, are much cheaper than in England; eggs run two for a penny, and tea you can purchase ridiculously cheaply, even so low as sixpence a pound. On the other hand, beer is a luxury that you will not drink in the jungles for less than eightpence or tenpence a pint, unless you get country-brewed, which is a little less expensive, and moderate in quality, and whisky will cost you four to five shillings a bottle. But soda-water is obtainable at sixpence or eightpence a dozen, and there is a manufactory in every considerable place where three or four Europeans reside. You can get good cigars for two shillings and eightpence to four shillings a hundred, but tobacco is dear.

Russian and American kerosene-oil is purchased by the five-gallon tin at about the same price as in England, and is the universal illuminant. Lamps are made especially for India, the ordinary English ones being of little use in the bungalow's large rooms, often with dark ceilings that absorb a great deal of light. I once took out half a dozen duplex-burner lamps from England, and discarded them all within a month, as they were utterly powerless to perform their purpose. All cooking is done by charcoal, and this is one of the heaviest expenses in the kitchen, as also is firewood if you happen to live in one of the untimbered districts.

The Anglo-Indian is, or should be, an early riser. To lie late in bed is called a "Europe morning." A cup of tea is always served when you are awakened, and as soon as you are dressed comes *chotahazri*, or the little breakfast, consisting of tea, toast, eggs, and fruit. The morning ride follows, and the most is made of the cool hours before eight or, at latest, nine o'clock. With the military, however, this is the busiest part of the day, being devoted to parades. But office men, by which you include most Government officials and all commercial men, have to breakfast at nine to reach their courts or offices in time for ten o'clock opening. Two is the hour for tiffin, often served at office; in fact, in some of the merchants' offices in Calcutta this meal is provided by the firm. Dinner is always as late as possible, for after sunset the gay and social part of the twenty-four hours begins. After dinner every one adjourns to the verandah, and stretches himself out in a lounge-chair to smoke, and, the process of digestion over, it is early to bed if you want a full night's sleep.

In the hot weather, it is customary to "shut up the bungalow" at about seven in the morning, when the temperature is moderately low in comparison with what it will rise to a few hours later. Every door and window is closed, and thereafter the greatest care taken to make entrances and exits as quickly as possible, for a door left open for any length of time soon raises the temperature. If kept carefully closed, it is remarkable how cool the room keeps compared with the heat out of doors. Thermantidotes and *tattis* are other devices for generating cool air, being a system of forcing a draught through wet screens of grass, which are cooled by the evaporation. They are delicious but dangerous. Water is cooled for drinking on the same principle (if ice is unprocurable), being placed in a porous earthenware vessel, and swung to and fro in the heated atmosphere, with the result that what was tepid and nauseous becomes sufficiently chilled. In old days, a special servant was kept, who was an expert at water-cooling, and did nothing else; but in modern days, few places except those off the line of rail are out of reach of ice, the price of which is within the range of even the natives, being retailed at about a halfpenny a pound.

Nothing strikes the English eye so much on first taking up residence in an Indian bungalow as the tameness of the bird and animal life that haunts it. The sparrows are in and out of all the rooms, and even build their nests in a chink of the ceiling. I have watched the most prodigious battles between a cock sparrow and his reflection in my mirror, and he and his kind are the most abandoned pilferers when the table is set for meals. The minah, or Indian starling, is tamer than the English robin, and a noisy nuisance, being engaged in permanent feuds with all his connections. The crow is a noted robber, and nothing is safe from him; leave a cutlet on a plate, and he will snatch it off in a twinkling. Kites swirl over the compound all day long, and make the sweeper's life a burden, watching over the chickens. Monkeys in some districts play havoc with your garden. The little grey squirrels are in and out of your verandah all day long, and ugly lizards bask in the sun on the floor, with occasional swift darts at a resting fly. All these are "shockingly tame." If the list of aliens in your premises ended here, you would not have much to complain of. But there are other and less agreeable inhabitants, such as snakes, scorpions, and centipedes. Spiders, too, of hideous dimensions, and rats, called "bandicoots," of gigantic size, and musk-rats, that leave an odour behind them most horrible. It is said, I believe with perfect truth, that a musk-rat running over a bottle of wine or soda-water will taint its contents. You seldom hear of Europeans being stung by snakes, scorpions, or centipedes; but the pests are, nevertherless, often numerous,—how common in some places, may be gathered from the fact that I have known a dog, that was particularly clever at the trick, to kill nine scorpions in my drawing-room in one evening, just after the bursting of the monsoon, when the creatures were swarming out of the cracks and crevices in which they had passed the hot weather. I have known only two cases of fatal snake-bites, both natives, during a period when I must have seen some thousands of the reptiles, and never without a shuddering horror I could never overcome. Lesser pests are found in the flying insects of the rainy season, smelly objectionables, and winged ants that swarm in millions, and, attracted by the light, seem to take a delight in flopping into your soup at dinner. Nor must white ants be forgotten, which perhaps do more damage than any other insect. They will eat away the bottom of a portmanteau, or the sole of a boot, in a single night, and they make it impossible to have boarded floors. Window frames and doorposts require to be periodically renewed, for you suddenly find them collapsing, and on examination discover they are perfectly hollow, having been burrowed into by white ants so artfully that only the thin skin of the surface is left intact. Fish-moths are a funny little insect, very like a silvery fish, that dine off your books, binding or inside, with impartiality. Rats and mice of the common English variety haunt your "go-down," and as nobody keeps cats in India, you are very much at their mercy. You are spared the ravages of the cat, only to find sometimes a worse thief in the mongoose, which, if it gets into your fowl-house, will kill every inmate, and drink its blood, and decamp. And for your water there are times when you have to beware of guinea-worms, and always of the microbes of dysentery and cholera. Fleas, *et hoc genus*, you cannot keep out of a house with its cement floors, and mats for them to find instant refuge in, and probably dogs enjoying the run of your rooms. In the rainy season, I have often suffered from a regular invasion of fleas, when they came into the house in legions and established themselves until fine weather set in, and then took it into their head to depart almost as unanimously as they entered. Lastly, the night brings with it bats, some of them harmless little fellows, but very irritating in your dining or drawing room; others, huge brutes, called flying foxes, that pillage your fruit trees. "The naturalist on the prowl" (to quote the title of a very entertaining Anglo-Indian book) will find plenty of subjects for investigation in and around the bungalow.

Looking back on Indian life, the one place in the bungalow that always recurs to my memory with pleasurable sensations is the verandah. There is nothing like it in English homes. There you always find the most comfortable armchairs, each with its small teapoy by its side to hold your peg-tumbler. With the chicks down, the glare kept out, and the sun round at the other side of the house, the shady verandah becomes the abiding-place. It is generally festooned with creeping flowers, and you can see to read in it without that straining required in the darkened drawing-rooms of Anglo-India. And it is inseparably associated with that delicious hour after dinner, so cool and sleepy and lazy, when you lay yourself out for perhaps the only part of the day free from positive physical discomfort. It has, too, many other associations; here your dogs, best companions of your lonely exile, lie and stretch themselves all day long; hither are your horses brought to receive their morning treat of bread or sugar-cane. From here you can loll and watch the sparrows and the squirrels and the minahs, and last, but not least, the crafty crows, that each and all "have a song to sing, oh!" if you can only understand their language, and enter into their idiosyncrasies. And here you receive your guests, if there is any intimacy between you and them, without stiff formality. I vow it is the pleasantest spot in Anglo-India; the one associated with its pleasantest moments, and to which memory recurs with just a *soupçon* of regret that in returning to England we have cut ourselves off from verandah life!

CHAPTER XVI

OUT-OF-DOOR LIFE

OUT-OF-DOOR life in India may be divided into three categories. First of all there is the life known as "going into camp," or "on tour," which many Government officials are obliged to follow during the cold weather in the execution of their ordinary duties; then the habitual open air employment of engineers, forest officers, planters, railway employees, and so forth; and lastly, out-of-door life in the shape of sport and recreation.

From the beginning of November to the end of February or March as much of Anglo-India as is able keeps in the open, to make up for those eight weary months of confinement, during which it has been imprisoned under punkahs and bottled up in bungalows. This is the season when the Government officials travel about their districts on inspection tour, which, to those who like riding and shooting, is the most enjoyable of all the various phases of duty.

Camping life is, indeed, a delightful institution of India. The itinerary of the district tour is mapped out, and preparations are made for a three or four months' gipsy existence under the skies, but accompanied with the refinement of comfort which the Anglo-Indian knows so well how to secure under such conditions; for tent-life has been brought to a high pitch of luxury. The camp equipage will consist of a big office tent, and a couple for dwelling in, with accommodation for the servants. There will be bullock-carts, or camels, to carry the baggage, including the most ingenious articles of camp-furniture, which can be telescoped or folded into portable dimensions. Indeed, you will sometimes see superimposed on a couple of camels a variety of beds, tables, chairs, and chests of drawers (these take into halves, and are slung one on each side), which, when opened and set out, suggest the requirement of a small pantechnicon van for their removal. Generally a portion of the poultry-yard is carried during these excursions, and a goat or two driven along to supply milk. And when the camp is pitched under a shady mango *tope*, or grove of trees, the *dhurries* or carpets laid, the ingenious collapsible furniture arrayed in its expanded usefulness, the camp-lamps shedding their bright glow within the tent, a crackling fire blazing in front of the door, why, there are very few habitations for which you would wish to change this travelling one.

The cold-weather tour of the head official of a district, who is in effect its governor, is a sort of triumphal progress. He lives on the fat of the land; at his nod transport and provisions of every description appear in plenty; for him, the best *khubber* where game is to be found, and beaters galore to drive it out of its haunts. At each halting-place the headman comes to offer him welcome, and the finest the village can afford, and all the ryots assemble to make their *salaams.* His tour is like an old English "visitation," and, if an energetic officer, he probably does more good in his district during these few cold weather months, when he is brought face to face with its requirements, than during the rest of the year. For they bring him into touch with the people in a way that can never occur in station life.

I know few people who fail to appreciate tent-life in India. It carries with it a sensation of its own of novelty, freedom, and movement. Here to-day, and there to-morrow! Away from the civilisation of the head station, and in a delightful atmosphere of unconventionality! Not until a man has spent several long months in office and bungalow can he fully realise the joy and relief of the plain and jungle, far transcending the pleasure of a seaside holiday in England, or a trip to the northern moors. And, best of all, camping out amalgamates duty with pleasure. What health, what spirits, what appetite it brings; all the rust of bungalow life is soon rubbed off, and the jaded palate, that has toyed with three nominal meals a day all through the burning hot weather and the steaming rains, now astonishes even its owner.

One is accustomed to associate tent-life in England with wet Wimbledons or blazing Bisleys, or excursions up river, and experiments in cooking that are generally unsuccessful. But they know how to do the thing better in India, where a camp conducted by experienced and expert servants is apt to astonish the new-comer. Do not imagine you rough it because you live in tents. Excepting that your roof is canvas, there is little difference between your comforts on tour and those in your bungalow. You will dine as well as in your dining-room, though your kitchen is nothing but a few stones grouped to support the cooking-pots under a tree. And you may reckon upon absolutely fine weather, with a temperature like the English climate in July or August, unless your fate takes you to some of the hotter districts. But, ordinarily speaking, no one goes out into camp until the temperature is in the pleasant stage.

If you are fond of shooting, there are few places where you cannot indulge in it. Shooting is perhaps the greatest charm of official camp-life. It is easy for the official, who in camp is entirely his own master, to arrange his office hours so as to permit of three or four hours with the gun. In the open country there is coursing also, and a couple of greyhounds will afford a pleasant variation of sport. An hour's stroll in the evening nearly always takes you for a round where you can add to your larder.

And then the pleasure of marching. You are going, let us say, to shift camp to-morrow. After dinner, your big dwelling-tent is struck and packed whilst you are enjoying your postprandial cheroot over the camp-fire, and, with its furniture, sent ahead to the next halting-place. Your sleeping-tent remains for you to spend the night in, and after early breakfast the next morning, you mount your horse and canter the ten or fifteen miles that have to be travelled, or perhaps shoot over a part of the ground, arriving at your new camp at ten or eleven o'clock, to find your tent pitched and a breakfast awaiting you, for the cook went on ahead after serving your dinner. By tiffin-time, your sleeping-tent will have arrived, and by three o'clock, except for the change of scene and surroundings, you will hardly tell that any alteration has been made in the encampment. And so you march, from place to place, always comfortable, never put out, and living with as much regularity as you would at home, except for that unpunctuality which is often a concomitant of shooting, when a long chase after a wounded quarry, or the seductions of a particularly hot field of quail, or well-stocked swamp of snipe, keep you abroad longer than you intended.

Take it for all in all, there is no phase of Anglo-Indian life so delightful as camping out. Whether it is the official on his rounds of duty, or the soldier on the route march from cantonment to cantonment, or the sportsman engaged in the pursuit he loves best, you may be sure one and all are enjoying themselves. For my own part, the happiest holidays I spent in my life were under canvas, and when I look back to those camping-days on the plains of Kattywar or the Punjab, in the jungles of the Ghauts and the Terai, or on the slopes of the Himalayas, I have an idea that I would change the civilisation of this congenial home-life for India again, if it only meant camping out and shooting!

Let us turn now to those whose duties are always more or less out of doors in India. I will pass over the soldier, because his career in cantonments is not an open air one except so far as the cooler morning hours are concerned, and in the cold weather he camps it during the relief season in much the same way as the civilian official. Saving when on active service, he is practically resident in his barracks or bungalow during those fierce noontide heats when exposure is trying.

Perhaps the hardest life of any lived by a European in India is that of the engine-driver on the railway. True, he gets remarkably good wages, two to three hundred pounds a year; but he earns them! In the hot weather it is by no means an unknown thing for an engine-driver to be found dead from heat apoplexy on his engine, and many European guards suffer in a lesser degree. And on the railway generally there is a constant exposure to the sun that makes it a far from enviable line of life.

Civil engineers in the Public Works Department have also a great deal of hot-weather outdoor work. It is a good season for building, and they are constantly called upon to inspect the works, such as roads, bridges, and canals, under their charge. For them, camp-life does not bear such a pleasant complexion as for some of their *confrères* in Government employ, and to keep well in touch with your district in May and June, and "slog at it" out of doors in a temperature of over a hundred in the shade, is apt to try the strongest man. Officials in the police suffer the same inconveniences, whilst the forest officer, the "jungle *sahib*," as he is called, is by the very nature of his occupation a man of the open. Such officials are practically touring nine or ten months out of the twelve, only housing up in the headquarters station during the monsoon months, when they do all their office work and annual reports.

Perhaps of all out-of-door workers the planters have the best time of it, especially those favoured ones who live in the "hills," like the planters of Darjeeling and the Neilgherries. Even under much less pleasant circumstances they get acclimatised, and there are old stagers in steaming Assam who vow it is one of the best climates in India. The tea-planters are the most numerous in this body, and are chiefly distributed over Northern and North-Eastern India, with a few in Travancore. In Southern India are the coffee-planters, confined practically to the Madras Presidency.

Indigo planting, whose home is in Bengal and Behar, is a decaying industry, but the life used to be reckoned the best of the three. All enjoy a holiday more or less in the cold weather, when work is slack.

Life on a tea plantation, when markets and seasons are favourable and the climate good, goes as near perfection as Anglo-Indian life may for a young and active man. The home is often a settled one, and that is a great factor in making yourself comfortable in an Indian bungalow. You furnish your house for living in, not for scrambling out of; you plant your garden with trees whose fruit you may legitimately hope to eat, and you settle down to make yourself comfortable. Unhappily, the good old days are past when prosperity was universal, and the modern tea-planter has to bear a heavy burden of anxiety under the altered conditions that have made the industry a precarious one.

Here is a description of a tea-planter's day on his estate. He is up before sunrise, and after a good *chotahazri*, to which he seems able to do better justice than most folk, off to his factory to take the morning reports and inspect the earlier stages of manufacture. This keeps him fully employed until nine o'clock, when he will jump on his horse and ride round the outdoor work, inspecting the gangs of coolies in the field until the eleven o'clock gong sounds to suspend work. Galloping back to his bungalow, he enjoys a bath, and sits down to the "planter's breakfast," which is not a mere bacon-and-eggs affair, but a *déjeuner à la fourchette*, with a reputation of its own. Often it is partaken of in the verandah, and is always an elaborate function round which the working-day revolves. Then comes the lounge in the long grasshopper verandah chair and the luxurious cheroot that has a better flavour than any other in the twenty-four hours, with, perhaps, forty winks to be winked, though as a rule the planter is far too busy in the hot weather to snatch a nap. About half-past twelve there is another visit to be paid to the factory and office, a court to be held at which administrative work is gone through, such as paying the men, giving out contracts, physicking the sick, and finally there comes the hot afternoon visit to the operations in the field, the most trying time of the whole day. At half-past four the planter knocks off, and may be considered to have done a fair day's *dág*, or work. Now comes recreation—lawn-tennis, a ride to visit a neighbour, or a walk with the dogs. This in the manufacturing season; in the cold weather, when the factory is shut, one round of the outdoor work generally suffices, and there are long afternoons to be spent in shooting, or playing cricket, or other sports in which many can find time to meet together and take a part. Sunset, with the short twilight of a southern land, terminates the afternoon all too soon, but not the pleasure, for now all collect in the verandah for pegs and pipes until dinner. Or perchance there is a piano in the bungalow, by no means an uncommon thing, and then there is a musical interlude, or, equally popular, a rubber of whist. But whatsoever form of diversion occurs, it is flavoured with "planters' hospitality," which has won a name for itself. After dinner there is little going on, for the planter as a rule falls asleep after a long day in the open, and if he manages a game of whist it will be as much as he cares to keep awake for, for he will get up at or before sunrise next morning.

A planter is an autocrat on his estate, and if he is lucky enough to live in a district where the labour is easily done, and what is more important, easily obtained, there is no man in India more free and independent. But of late years, a cloud has hovered over the planting industry, and the "good times" for indigo, tea, or coffee have gone by. "Economy" is the cry, and a cutting down of salaries, never munificent, the result—in some cases to the extent of half the former emoluments. Indian planting was a fine opening once for energetic youth, without much brains; it is so no longer, even if the youth has brains as well as energy.

Lastly, in this review of out-of-door life in India, we come to sport and recreation, and here is a feast of good things. The Europeans in the East enter with a peculiar zest, both from enthusiasm and because of the benefit that comes from physical exercise into sports that take them out of their bungalows. I suppose the game of lawn-tennis has done more for the average Anglo-Indian than all the drugs in the pharmacopœia. I have seen men playing it in the height of the hot season, with a turkish-bath towel hung on a pole just outside the court, the condition of which at the end of a set was eloquent of some evil humours expelled from the body. Tennis is a game adapted for the limited society of an up-country station, and one in which ladies can not only join, but in India, from constant practice, become almost as proficient as men. The courts are very hard as a rule, many being made of beaten earth, and the game requires a display of far more agility than when played on grass.

Cricket is indulged in a good deal in the cold weather, on very fast pitches as a rule. It is particularly popular amongst the military, for in civil society it is not often feasible to get up a full game. But in a cantonment there are often a grand series of matches through the winter. Football is not unfrequently played in the rainy season, when the temperature is most trying, and the energy and enthusiasm shown under such circumstances speak eloquently for its popularity. The inter-regimental Football Challenge Cup gives rise to an exciting competition; in fact, for the keenest rivalry in purely English games you have always to go to a cantonment. Otherwhere, except in the big cities, the population is too small to supply full sides for cricket or football.

Racing has been the favourite sport in India from time immemorial for those who can afford it, but, of recent years, the rich rajahs have stormed the turf, and monopolised all the prizes. There are, however, a large number of "sky meetings," as they are called, where the man of small means, who loves the sport for the sake of the horse, is able to enter his own nag and ride it, and at these, if the business is less imposing, the fun is none the less. The *gymkhana* meet, which is a purely local affair, gives the amateur a field day, and brings the pastime within reach of all, and as every one owns a "gee," and riding is a universal accomplishment, the "scurry stakes" appeal to all. Nor are these *gymkhanas* limited to racing, but are an *olla podrida* of all sorts of sports, and you can spend an exceedingly entertaining afternoon at them, engaging in, or looking on, a variety of competitions which include tent-pegging, lime-cutting, and kindred exhibitions of skill on horseback, for the art of equitation enters largely into all sportive gatherings.

Polo is a very favourite game in India, as may well be imagined in a country where every subaltern keeps a horse, and has not the slightest objection to risking his neck. No military cantonment and but few of the larger stations are without their polo ground, and there is always a "polo evening" once or twice a week. The caricaturist who is good at horses with his pencil will find many humours on the Indian polo field, where men with slender purses play the game on the same long-suffering animals they ride in the morning, and trap in the middle day, and whose original cost may not have exceeded a ten-pound note. For you can get a very passable country-bred nag for that sum, and for twenty pounds a mount you need not be ashamed to be seen striding. Some of the hill ponies will give you extraordinary value for money. I remember buying one for six pounds that I rode every day for twelve years, and he was good enough to give away but too good to shoot at the end of that period. But that was up in the Himalayas, and the same pony would probably have commanded three times the price in the plains. I have owned perhaps a score of what are called "plantation ponies," and never gave more than twenty pounds for the best of them; several of the cheaper ones carried me forty and forty-five miles a day.

If I have left pig-sticking and shooting to the last, it is certainly not because they are the least in the sporting pleasures of India. The former is accounted the finest of all field sports, and takes the place of hunting in England, with the additional advantage of being within the reach of many who could never afford to ride to hounds at home. The sport is fostered by "tent clubs," which are practically camping-out clubs, and Sunday is perhaps the most popular day for a meet. The members ride out to a pre-arranged camp on the Saturday afternoon, hunt all Sunday, and are back at their stations on Monday in time for office or parade. The sport dates from the eighteenth century, and the old term of the "fraternity of pig-stickers" still holds good, for there is a veritable brotherhood amongst those who follow this entrancing method of hunting.

Last of all comes shooting, which I may call the universal sport of India. Poor in resources is that Anglo-Indian who does not possess a gun. The game is free to all to shoot, the only restriction being a "close" season, and, in some districts, a regard for the prejudices of the natives.

Thus peacocks in many places and *neilghai*, or wild cattle, are accounted sacred, and, in fact, so tame, owing to immunity from chase, that no sportsman would shoot them. The former may be seen sunning themselves on the village walls, and the *neilghai* is a privileged despoiler of crops, who has never experienced anything more dreadful than a hoot. Tiger-shooting is the sport of the wealthy, for it entails a heavy expenditure in elephants, beaters, and general arrangements. Jungle *hånking* for big game, such as sambre, deer, and animals which require to be driven towards the guns out of thick jungle, also costs a considerable amount, for although beaters are only paid twopence or threepence a day per head, when you have to engage them in regiments, it is prudent to tot up the outlay. But antelope stalking in the plains is open to most people at the expense of a railway fare—you may occasionally see the buck as you pass through the wilder parts of the country in the train—and can be combined with small-game shooting. The railways have, however, done much to exterminate the antelope in many parts of India, and render them very wild. I remember, thirty years ago, shooting in Kattywar, and seeing herds of many hundreds of buck where nowadays ten are quite difficult to come across. It is the same with the more savage wild animals. In my plantation was a ravine called the "Wolves' nullah," from the wolves that once swarmed in it; but not one has been seen there for twenty years.

It is, however, the small game that never fails to give sport. Partridge, hare, snipe, wild-duck, and quail are open to almost any Anglo-Indian who takes the trouble to look for them. There is no fun equal to snipe and quail shooting for the amount of blazing away it gives you, and both birds are excellent for the table, which is more than you can say for Indian game in general. Few sports surpass duck-shooting, if you get into a good spot, and, after the woodcock, the mallard is about the best eating bird in India. I do not think English people realise how easily Indian shooting is to be enjoyed. In 1874, I made a sporting trip to India for six months, and after deducting two for the voyage, much slower then than it is now, had four months as good sport as any one could desire, and, big and small, killed about three thousand head of game. The entire cost of the trip was under two hundred pounds; but I "gipsy'd" it in camp, knocking about with a single small tent, one horse, and a couple of camels. Two or three going together could accomplish such a trip nowadays as economically, and if "furloughs" in England were as long and as common as in India, I could not imagine a better way of spending them than three or four months' camping under an Indian sky.

The out-of-door recreations of city life in India need little description. There is something of the cockney in the Anglo-Indian who lives in Calcutta or Bombay. A ride is generally the limit of his outdoor exercise, and he "Rotten-rows" it as gingerly as you may see in Hyde Park. More frequently the limit of his horsemanship is the bandstand, where he lolls in his saddle, or nerves himself for a walk by strand or seashore. In Bombay, there is a good deal of yachting, and in the swift-sailing lateen-rigged boats, it is passing pleasant to spend an evening in the harbour, and better still to take an extended trip up some of the creeks. But the more strenuous exercises always gave me the more pleasure and profit, and I look back to the days I spent in jungle and jheel, with rifle and gun, a couple of good nags to carry me afield, and a leash of greyhounds to encourage me to a gallop after a jackal now and again, I look backward to those with a sigh, as I find myself surrounded with the bricks and mortar of London, and recognise that there are some phases of Anglo-Indian out-of-door life you cannot duplicate in England, wish you ever so hard. If Eastern exile were all composed of camp-life, very few would care to terminate it until overtaken by that fatal ailment called *Anno Domini.*

CHAPTER XVII

SEPIA SURROUNDINGS

THE Anglo-Indian cannot escape from the tyranny of the brown skin. There is no privacy in India; the fierce glare that beats upon a throne is hardly less inquisitorial than the quiet glances of apparently mild brown eyes directed at the unconscious Anglo-Indian unceasingly.

The magnificent staff of native servants, about which so much has been written and remarked, is, in effect, a staff of spies. There is no escape from them, and from the time that you tumble out of bed in the morning to the hour when you turn in again, you are never free from the sensation of "somebody there." Even through the silent night hours the periodical cough of the punkah coolie serves to remind you of the ever-watchful presence. You live in a perpetual *qui vive*, for amidst these sepia surroundings you know you are the conspicuous object.

By nature, natives are a most inquisitive folk, and India is a land of *gup*, which is the vernacular for gossip. Whatever you do, say, and (I was almost adding) think, is reported, and whatever happens in your bungalow becomes common information to your neighbours. Anglo-Indians, and especially their wives, are in many cases confirmed gossips. The *ayah*, or lady's-maid, has a genius for disseminating scandal, and I have been led to believe that more tittle-tattle is talked during the hour when the hair of Anglo-Indian womankind is being brushed than at any other of the twenty-four. Nor can I acquit the masculine sex of freedom from a similar curiosity, for it often displays a distinct partiality for listening to the *gup* of the barber, or the babblings of the bearer who dresses his master.

And here, in passing, I may make a note of the lazy and luxurious habits into which sepia surroundings seduce the Anglo-Indian, and the royal way in which he adapts himself to being waited upon. There are many little personal offices in India which it is derogatory to perform for yourself, and the extension of this leads to the performance of several others by proxy. No one, for instance, laces up his own boots, or carries a parcel, or undertakes anything in the nature of an errand, and I have seen Europeans walking in the rain with natives to carry their umbrellas over them. But it is in his dressing-room that this peculiar trait in the Anglo-Indian character is emphasised. Many a man reverts to the habits of his childhood, and practically allows his bearer to dress him. His vest and shirt are held open for him to slip his head and shoulders into, the passage of his trousers is simplified, his socks and shoes are put on for him, and assistance with his *cummerbund*, or waistband, follows as a matter of course. It is sometimes really ludicrous to see young fellows, a few months in the country, adapt themselves to these Sybaritic idiosyncrasies! As for old stagers, they really become almost as helpless as infants, and will employ the barber to cut their toenails. After a day's shooting, the sportsman's feet are usually washed by his faithful attendant, and the brushing and folding of clothes are performances that the average Englishman in India forgets how to accomplish.

If you do not find privacy in the dressing-room, you can hardly be free from espionage in the rest of the bungalow, where it is chronic. The verandah is guarded by the *chupprassi*, who squats or stands there to run errands, carry letters (there are no messages despatched in India, where all communications are sent by *chits*, which is the anglicised and abbreviated Hindustani for "notes"), and act generally the part of a human bell. In Egypt, you "clap hands, clap hands till somebody comes;" but in India, you lift up your voice and shout, which is sometimes inconvenient and often irritating. By the word you use, you reveal to which Presidency you belong. If you belong to Bengal, you cry, *Koi hai?* which means, "Is anybody there?" if to Bombay, the summons is for "Boy!" The *chupprassi* is the chief of spies. Lesser ones are the gardener, who keeps his eye upon you as you lounge in the verandah; the groom, who attends you when you are out riding, and is an athletic runner; the *kitmudghar*, who waits behind your chair at table, and the native clerks who squat round your feet at office. Try how you will, you cannot get away from the native; he is "in the air," so to speak, and you come at last to resign yourself to a species of tyranny that completely robs you of the charm of solitude. It is an atmosphere difficult to realise in England, where an Englishman's home is his castle; in India, the bungalow is a combination of a conservatory and observatory.

And what makes this state of things so anomalous is that there is no assimilation between black and white. They are, and always must remain, races foreign to one another in sentiment, sympathies, feelings, and habits. Between you and a native friend there is a great gulf which no intimacy can bridge—the gulf of caste and custom. Amalgamation is utterly impossible in any but the most superficial sense, and affinity out of the question.

Nor in its material sense is affinity desirable. Without wishing to say anything offensive about my black brother, I must protest that when the atmosphere is too redolent of him and the unguents with which he anoints himself, he is decidedly objectionable, and there are times, many times, when it is as well that he should not get between you and the breeze. It is a delicate subject to dwell on, but decidedly one of the drawbacks of too "close" sepia surroundings. I will only instance a single illustration. It is one of the anomalies of railway travelling in India that whilst third-class carriages are reserved for the "poor-white," the first- and second-class passengers have no guarantee against the intrusion of gentlemen of colour whose domestic and social habits are not in accord with our ideas of delicacy of behaviour. There are native "compliments" after a hearty meal which are simply disgusting to an Anglo-Saxon; and nature did not build the white man and black on suitable lines to hugger-mugger it in a small saloon on a railway, which may be their mutual abode for two or three days. I am not exaggerating when I say that the presence of a native in the same carriage with you doubles the disgust one feels for a long, hot, and trying journey in a small, stuffy space.

Let us turn to another and less unpleasant aspect of the sepia. It is particularly conspicuous in office life, where all clerical work is performed by educated natives. A civilian's office is manned with Hindu and Mahomedan scribes, and all the "writers" in a commercial house are natives. That they make industrious machines no one can deny; but they are apt to be trying to the temper at times, and require an extraordinarily alert check kept on their manœuvres and blunders. Once get them outside their routine of work, and occasion them to draw on their imagination, and the result is disastrous. They cannot be used for correspondence, for they think on an entirely different plane from that of the European, and their eccentricities of composition are phenomenal. "Baboo English," as it is called, is often more comical than Mark Twain. It revels in polysyllabics and lexicographers' terms; straightforward English is a great deal too simple for the Baboo, and single syllable words are insufficient to show off his learning. "So much for your boasted British jurisprudence!" was the crushing commentary fired off by one indignant Baboo when an Englishman accidentally trod on his toes in a crowd. A European out shooting peppered a villager with snipe shot, and compensated him with ten rupees. In order to retain a written record of the transaction, he ordered his clerk to obtain a receipt for the money, and the phraseology the native wit hit on was, "To compounding one bloody murder, ten rupees. Omissions excepted." "Sir," wrote another of these clerkly originalities, "pray excuse from office this day on account of boil on left elbow as per margin," and illustrated the tumour, to scale, on the side of the sheet. Letters in this style are common in India, where the sepia thinks the Englishman much better approached by epistle, and hires scribes to write "petitions" detailing complaints or aspirations. Tl · professional letter-writer is an established and well-patronised functionary in India.

I have no doubt the other side of the picture,

which shows the mistakes English folk make in expressing themselves in the native languages, can display just as many comicalities if they were brought to notice. *Meem-sahib-bát*, or the ladies' rendering of the vernacular is notoriously unconventional, and Tommy Atkins speaks a lingo of his own which nobody outside a regimental bazaar can understand. The Indian *Charivari*, an attempt at an Oriental *Punch*, which has long ceased to exist, enshrined in its pages many gems of Anglo-Hindustani. But it is against the code of a native's etiquette to laugh, much less to deride, and he allows such lapses to pass without a change in his sober countenance. Very rarely he is unconsciously sarcastic, as when a European calls him "the son of a pig" (a too common formula of abuse), and he meekly rejoins, "Your honour is my father and my mother!" which is the commonest metaphor of compliment. But hilarity is foreign to the native character, and if he is surprised into a smile he will bend his face and relieve himself of it with a hand veiling his mouth.

In living amongst natives, as many Europeans have to do, it is necessary to attune your mind to theirs. India is a land of lies, inhabited by peoples who express a virtuous indignation against lying. It is also a land of unconscious exaggeration, for a native has the poorest idea of assessing things correctly, and in all information you receive you must make an allowance. If you are travelling and ask a wayfarer how far it is from your destination, he will, in all probability, assure you "one *kos*," a distance that answers to our mile, though it sometimes extends to two and a half. The place may be ten *kos* distant, but the formula remains the same, and until you begin to fall into the native's ways of thought and usage, you will meet with many bitter disappointments in trusting too implicitly to his word, and especially his ideas of computation. In this particular respect there is no one who can compete with the *shikari*, or man hired to show you the haunts of game. The roseate hues of early dawn, which predict tigers considerably over twelve feet from nose to tip of tail, blackbuck with thirty-inch horns, and snipe like locusts, if credited, fade into grey chagrin later in the day. It is not so much lying in many cases as an inability to speak the truth; in other words, the speaker tells you what he thinks is the case, when as a matter of fact he is depicting what he wishes it may be. He does it not unkindly, if you could only appreciate his line of reasoning. "What was the size of the wild-boar?" you ask of one who has come in with news of pig. "That size," is the reply, the horizontal hand indicating the altitude of a full-grown donkey. If you bid the man reflect and indicate again, he will, as likely as not, increase the height.

Sepia surroundings sometimes bring serious nuisances with them. In the most fashionable part of Bombay is situated the Hindu burning-ground, whereof ladies returning from the band-stand often have olfactory proofs. Conceive the scandal it would occasion in England if one of the principal thoroughfares were tainted with the smell of roasting human flesh! In the capital of Western India, you sniff suspiciously, shudder out an "Ugh!" cram your pocket-handkerchief to your nose, and there is an end of it. It is a custom of the country. Then, again, the native contaminates water with a most disgusting unconcern, washing himself in the tank from which you may be obliged to draw your drinking supply, and defiling it in sundry ways. I have alluded to the native's scantiness of attire; it is certainly something to shock, and a man taking his bath in public, with nothing on him but an exceedingly diminutive loin-cloth, is a common wayside spectacle. In parts of Southern India, the women are undraped from the waist upwards, the survival of an old custom which decreed it as an incentive to matrimony. All along the seaboard, you may put it that the female costume transgresses the laws of Occidental decency. Many of the lepers and beggars whom you see infesting the public highways are such loathsome sights that they would not be permitted abroad in civilised communities; and the cruelty to animals habitually practised in overworking them is a constant disgrace. Bullocks whose tails have practically been twisted off are exceedingly common, and the saddle sores and girth galls of horses and mules employed as pack animals, or in wheeled vehicles, make you shudder.

Minor nuisances are many. Nothing is more distracting to the nerves than the tom-toming that goes on all through the night when marriages or other festivals are in progress. What are the intermittent concerts of tom-cats on the tiles to the prolonged and maddening monotony of a single dull note repeated at short intervals, making night hideous? Then there are native caste prejudices which create inconvenience. In some Hindu districts, where the slaughter of kine is prohibited, it is impossible to get beef. For nearly twenty years, off and on, I never tasted it between February and October, and have sent seventy miles for a Christmas sirloin, and had it brought up by men on foot, relieving each other in relays. A mere trifle, you may think; but it becomes a little trying when you live on a diet of mutton and fowl every day for many months. Pork flesh, be it ham or bacon, you know to be unclean to your Mahomedan servants, and eat it "with all risks," as the auctioneers say. Under the same category, curiously enough, comes turkey, accounted a relation of the pig by the followers of the Prophet, because it carries a little rosette of bristles on its breast, though this may be news to the general.

In another part of these pages, I have mentioned the system of *dàlis*, or complimentary offerings. At Christmas these assume the form of an epidemic. Here the sepia has you on hip and thigh, for the system of the Christmas-box brings East and West into line at once. It is a moot question whether the word "box" may not be derived from *bucksheesh*, often abbreviated into "bux" in the colloquial. In India, the Christmas-box is a reciprocal function; all your servants and hangers-on and understrappers seize the opportunity to present you with a *dàli*, which you cannot very well decline. And, of course, when a native tips you, you must tip him back, and return nothing less respectable than silver for his copper. The *dàli*, with its little heap of sugar candy and rice, flowers and fruit, costs but a few pence at the utmost, and the procession of these gifts only finds a termination in the number of those who conceive that now is the time to make a good investment. They come and come, and, with a sickly smile and sullen eye, you *salaam* and submit yourself to the craftily disguised blackmail of Christmas *bucksheesh*, inwardly cursing the accumulation of sour oranges, and the ascending pile of sugar-candy, and the hillock of rice as it expands into a young mountain, and consigning Christmas customs to the same inferno to which you habitually consign native ones.

Consign them, and yet too often accommodate yourself to them! Things which you know to be constructively wrong you acquiesce in, and condone methods which are obsolete fetishes. Take the Indian *ayah*, or lady's-maid; she is in nine cases out of ten of the scavenger caste! No fastidious Englishman will touch a sweeper or scavenger, and yet he allows his wife to be waited on by a woman of the same low breed. You can hardly believe it, but it is the "custom," and the husband is often valeted by a high-caste Brahmin or Rajpoot who would decline to tread on the same carpet as the *ayah!* Of all the anomalies and topsy-turvies of Anglo-Indian domestic economy, this has always struck me as the most remarkable in its surrender to caste prejudice and sexual inferiority. Look at your horse, hobbled by the hind leg as well as haltered; that is a custom of the country which many people in England would denounce as cruel. But you will find it adopted in most Indian stables, because it has been handed down by the forefathers of your groom as the proper way to secure a horse. Observe the domestic utensils in common use in an Anglo-Indian's house; the *gurrah*, which (*pace* Sir George Birdwood) is like a wobbling football filled with water, is permitted to survive when a water-can would be infinitely more convenient to fill your bath with. And those copper cooking-pots, which can so easily become poisonous, remain in use because your cook prefers them! Can any one conceive a more clumsy device than the punkah for creating an artificial draught, with two coolies permanently attached to it? And yet we are only just beginning in the centres of civilisation to adopt electric fans and other substitutes suggested by Western ingenuity. The British have occupied India for a hundred and fifty years, and have left the building of their houses to the native architect, whose ideas have not changed since the times of Clive and Warren Hastings. The Indian bungalow is a century behind the age, but it is fashioned according to a hoary old custom, and we remain content with it. I know only one house in India designed on an English model, but with the addition of verandahs; it was called the "Folly." I must myself plead guilty to having built three bungalows, all on native lines, and I cannot explain why, except that it was the custom. Even in this age of cheap Swedish and Japanese matches, if you call for a light for your cheroot in Bombay, you will be supplied with a piece of glowing charcoal between a pair of tongs, because that is the method adopted in lighting the native hookah. The palanquin, carried by native bearers, still survives in the metropolitan cities, although it is as antiquated as the sedan chair, and more awkward to get out of than a social scrape. Yet a pious custom helps it to linger on in an age of motor-cars! But I could go on indefinitely multiplying these immutable mysteries of Asia that link us with the Georgian period in the economy of daily life; these tinder-boxes and elastic-side boots, as it were, used and worn under the dominion of the Emperor Edward the Seventh! And side by side with them, you have the intensely Western spectacle of a Hindu running to catch a suburban train, or a Mahomedan reporting the tramway conductor because he omitted to punch the penny-fare ticket!

The moral influence of sepia surroundings on the life of an Anglo-Indian is another matter altogether, and of this I have left myself little space to write. There is no doubt that the atmosphere puts a man's character to the test; some come out of it well, some uncommonly badly. The Anglo-Indian, be he ever so humble, finds many humbler beings to bow before him. The loafer on the highway has no need to shoulder the black man off his path, who voluntarily makes way for him. As you ascend in the social scale, this servility increases, and the sepia is ever metaphorically grovelling in the dust to the white complexion. It is not a wholesome atmosphere to live in, this conscious sense of social superiority, and is apt in some cases to turn heads. The Anglo-Indian becomes arrogant, quick-tempered, and impatient. He loses the knack of saying "Thank you," and acquires that of *bahaduring*, which is the importation of imperialism into private life. He is always "My lord" or "Your honour" to the native, or, for a variation, "Protector of the poor!" or "Cherisher of the needy!" Do you wonder that the Anglo-Indian becomes puffed-up? That he thinks more of himself than is compatible with his gifts and attributes? That he becomes curt in his treatment of the sepia? Such is not unfrequently the case, and an undue exploitation of "side" is a weak point in the Anglo-Indian's character. A six-months' furlough to the Colonies of Australia should be included in the curriculum of his life to negative the ill-effects of sepia surroundings and sepia servility.

CHAPTER XVIII

THE GLAD CRY

WHAT are the *pros* and what the *cons* of Anglo-Indian life, and to which side does the balance incline? I think I can strike it at once in the words of the familiar song, *Home, Sweet Home.* But there are two good columns of debtor and creditor considerations on either side before we arrive at it, and to some of these I will address myself.

The Anglo-Indian does not take his pleasures sadly, and, speaking generally, manages to have a good time of it during his period of exile. There is no place like India for gaiety and amusement, and no society which lays itself out more thoroughly for enjoyment. Within the short limits of the cooler evening hours, a vast amount of outdoor revelry is squeezed in. I do not speak of the cities, where there are large communities and amusement is conducted on a colossal scale, but of the petty out-stations which, weather permitting, become the headquarters of enjoyment, and in this respect contrast favourably with the dulness of life in English rural towns and villages.

In fact, they compare rather with those places in England which are called pleasure resorts. The reason is not far to seek; there is little of the English stiffness in Anglo-Indian society; everybody knows everybody else; and the hours of recreation are of necessity the same for all. Moreover, it often happens that there is only one meeting-place where the Europeans foregather with regularity and punctuality. These conditions bring people together, and having grouped themselves, they proceed to make the most of it. A similar system in England, that assembled acquaintances at a stated hour and for a stated time every day, would probably show the same results.

Then hospitality is universal in India, and dinner parties, dances, balls, private theatricals, and evening entertainments are far commoner than in England. This, again, is not to be wondered at, for you have servants to do everything for you. The commissariat is a simple affair relegated to your major-domo, and a Cinderella dance or garden-party comes within the means of many. Nor should I forget to mention that the racecourse, the polo ground, the cricket pitch, and the tennis courts cost practically nothing for their use, being Government lands allotted to every station for the benefit of the European community. In short, amusement is made easy in India, and the expense of a trifling subscription will make you free of everything.

Nor is India without its pleasure resorts, where

the fun is fast and furious. The Hill Stations in the hot weather are places where little else but gaiety and amusement is talked of or indulged in. Here are gathered together the fair sex, who cannot stand the heat of the baking plains, and hither flock men of all sorts and conditions "on leave" from their several duties. English novel readers know a good deal about Indian Hill Stations, which form the background of so much fiction; but apart from this not very wholesome atmosphere of flirtation and intrigue there is much that is harmless and happy. I do not know any sense of relief and delight greater than that of breathing in the mountain air after a long spell of the stifling heat below, or any scene more grateful to the eyes than the verdure of the hills and the panorama of distant snows after the drab monotony of the dusty plains. It is better than the sea to a Londoner, the Highlands to a Glasgow man. For it means something more than health; it brings a certain rejuvenisation of physical and mental energy. The cool wind soughing through the firs, the nights that require a blanket, the days that can be enjoyed out-of-doors instead of only survived under a punkah—these are things that make a run up to the hills the greatest treat of Anglo-Indian life.

Ladies find a compensation for their lonely Indian days in the gaiety of the evening hours. Although they are no longer all reckoned princesses, as was the case in the good old times, and may not always be able to fill their ball programmes, they have little cause to complain. For Anglo-India is very attentive to its womankind, and ladies are admitted to not a few of its clubs. And although the girl who goes out to find a husband may not be so uniformly successful as were her foremothers thirty years ago, I fancy there are few "spins"—if they are still "spins"—who look back to the life they spent in India without pleasurable feelings, even should the campaign have been a failure from a matrimonial point of view.

To the man who loves hunting, riding, and shooting, India is an ideal land. What are luxuries confined to the rich in England become every one's property in the East. For myself, I always associate sport with my pleasantest recollections of exile. No holidays since those of one's schooldays can compare to the Christmas week, or fortnight, spent in camp, shooting and riding. I can call to mind many such, when with four or five genial companions we cut ourselves adrift from railways and roads, and lived the gipsy life. Dear are the memories of the snug tents pitched under the shady mango *topes;* the morning gallop and the midday sport; the evening stroll with a shotgun; the dinner partaken under a green canopy, with the camp-fire roaring and brightening up the scene, and the chairs drawn around it presently for sing-songs or discussions of the varied adventures of the day.

Another advantage of Anglo-Indian life is that money goes further and provides more in certain directions. People naturally go to India to improve their circumstances, and you may say, in a general way, every one is better off than he would have been in England. Even the man on small means can get a vast amount of pleasure and comfort out of his income, and there is but little of that struggle which we associate with genteel poverty. Taken all round, the Anglo-Indian is a well-to-do individual, and if his ship is not sailing smoothly, it is mostly his own fault. The scale of salaries is arranged on a far more liberal basis than in England, and "dreadfully poor" folk are only so in comparison with the dreadfully rich ones.

And, to most people, the object attainable is satisfactory. The civilian has opportunities of great distinction open to him, and more rewards and decorations than in any other civil service under the Crown. The soldier sees plenty of camp-life, and the fortunate one a full share of fighting, and is not the poor man, financially speaking, he remains in other outposts of the Empire. The merchant has a prospect of a quick fortune, and professional men—doctors, barristers, dentists, and experts generally—make a larger income than they would in England. Mechanics enjoy handsome wages, and "poor whites" are rare, and chiefly confined to the loafing class, whose misfortunes you may trace to intemperance. The missionary lives a far from arduous life, and the chaplain is the best paid clergyman in the church, with a pension of a pound a day after a comparatively short term of service. For his cloth, indeed, there is nobody better off than the Anglo-Indian "padre." And you may say of the Anglo-Indian generally, he is a prosperous man, and judge it by the way he grumbles when he returns to England, and misses all the luxuries of Indian life.

The climate is, of course, the great drawback, and yet sometimes when I get climate-cursed in England I think not unkindly of the hottest days I ever spent in India. The skies were blue, at least, and when it did rain it rained to some purpose. Englishmen grumble under any circumstances, and do so with undeviating regularity against the heat of the East; and yet, I think, not so much as at the perverse variability and cosmopolitan detestability of English meteorological conditions. For when the weather is a fixed equation you can circumvent it, and do in a measure, in India; but when it shifts and changes, as it does in England, you can in practice do nothing but swear at it. And put east wind and London fog against hot winds and monsoon vapour, and I honestly prefer the latter.

As regards the quality and strenuousness of work, the Englishman cannot, does not, and is not called upon to do as much in India as at home. In commercial life, the office hours are from ten to five; but there are many more holidays than in England. In a country where there are three creeds, each with its festivals to be observed, there are three sets of holidays, and the *Doorga Poojahs* supply a week straight off the reel. In Government employ, Sundays and festivals account for almost a third of the year. Then, again, you seldom see the Anglo-Indian bustling. If you go into a shop or office in the larger cities, there is a distinctly placid air, which argues no high amount of pressure. The tiffin hour is an oasis that occupies a big slice in the day, and I have known business men nap in their chairs, under the drowsy influence of the punkah. Another point to be remembered is that nearly all the uninteresting clerical work in India is done by native clerks. It is true the civilian is rather surfeited with writing reports, and I have heard dignitaries of the administration, with inky fingers, swearing at the bureaucratic head centre for its appetite for unnecessary details. But over his more practical duties the same high functionary may often be observed with a cheroot or cigarette in his mouth. In fact, nearly all Europeans smoke in their offices, and this habit faithfully reflects what I may call the sauntering ease of Eastern life. Military men are notoriously unemployed during the hot weather months, and the enforced idleness of barrack bounds is the greatest curse of Tommy Atkins's Indian career. The artisan classes are by no means driven, except on the railway, and there is a decided "consideration" shown to everybody which allows the Anglo-Indian a great deal of latitude, not to say lassitude, in the execution of his duties. Moreover, there is the ever-present native to serve him and be at his beck and call. Sepia surroundings are often a nuisance, but on occasions mightily convenient. Sometimes, when I look at the kitchen-midden heap that constitutes my writing-table in this land of civilisation, I sigh for my *duftri*, who used to tidy my desk twice daily in India, wipe my pens, fill my inkpots, set me out a new sheet of blotting-paper every day, array my writing-paper and envelopes, copy my letters in the press, fold and enclose them in their covers, and finally weigh and stamp each! Not to mention altering the date-rack, killing flies, abusing the *punkah-wallah* when he failed to create a strong draught, preparing a "peg," advising me of the time, acting as a notebook to remind me of things to be done, and, so far as my personal comfort went, thinking for me when I was too lazy to think for myself!

Occupation for occupation I would sooner be a European working in India than in England, and to sum the matter up generally I should call Indian life, in its working aspect, a "jolly easy one," with many compensations to make up for local drawbacks of climate.

Having thus sketched in broadest outline the advantages of the Indian life, a few words must be devoted to its disadvantages, without necessity to refer again to the climate except to point out the lassitude to which it gives rise, and the disinclination for work which it engenders. I know few things more trying than the obligation to carry out duties when all energy is gone, and the task that under ordinary circumstances would yield satisfaction, if not pleasure, in its accomplishment, becomes an effort of compulsion very like slavery. Lassitude is not necessarily laziness; it is a running down of the system, a condition of mind and body for which the man who suffers from it cannot be blamed. It incapacitates, and makes work a "grind." As a rule, I think Anglo-India grinds a great deal at its work. There are weeks and months when the Anglo-Indian does not enjoy the happiness of a *mens sana in corpore sano*, which is so essential to the proper conduct of the affairs of life. A man suffering from a chronic headache or permanent lumbago is not the individual to solve acrostics or dig the garden; the disabilities of lassitude are, in their way, just as great, and it requires the exercise of no common amount of will-power to "buckle-to," when all the starch has been melted out of the system, and mind and body are in a limp, negative state.

Partly arising from climate, partly from circumstances, comes the question of health. Ill-health is one of the drawbacks of life in the East. The liver is a permanent misery, and many other ills to which man's flesh is heir follow close on its heels. A great number of Anglo-Indians suffer from chronic complaints who would assuredly have escaped their afflictions in England. It is a trite observation to say that good health is the greatest of all blessings, and yet it is not until you begin to have experience of sickness that this elementary truth is realised. In a planting life in the jungles, it is especially trying. In the district wherein I lived, I remember over a dozen Europeans dying without medical aid, and in not a few cases from preventable causes. Three succumbed to cholera, and were dead before the doctor, who lived over twenty miles away, could gallop in. It is dreadful to think of life so needlessly squandered, and when the bitterness is brought home to you by seeing your own friends passing away, and yourself unable to help them, it is hard to bear. Moreover, the funeral has to follow death so immediately in the East that it hardly seems decent. You may be called on to bury a man with whom you were lunching the day before, and experiences like these score a deep mark in the recollection. But the saddest memory of all is the Indian cemetery, with its crowded, uncouth, masonry monuments, and its general air of desolation and abandonment. In India, the dead are not treated well, and it is one of the disgraces of British administration. In the humblest English village churchyards you will see more respect and attention paid to the resting-places of the departed than is paid to the tombs of many of the heroes who helped to win India for Great Britain. Indian cemeteries are hideous with neglect, and in some of the out-of-the-way, up-country stations are even given over to the jungle and wild beasts.

However, this has little to do with life in India. We are talking of its drawbacks, and chief amongst these must be placed the perennial partings between husbands and wives, parents and children. In England, man and wife hardly know what it is to dwell apart; in India, it is a common condition of matrimonial life for four months in the year, when wives have to be sent up to the Hill Stations. But this, again, is a far less unhappy state of affairs than that other alternative of sending wife and family home to England. The sorrow of separation from all he holds most dear hangs over the Anglo-Indian, and makes his life one clouded with constant and prolonged partings. And I think it is from this phase of it that India has been called the Land of Regrets.

But there is another species of separation I must mention, and that is the exclusion from civilisation which a life in the jungles entails. In the selection of his career, the Anglo-Indian cuts himself off from much that goes to elevate life in the West. He is out of touch with art and literature, and seldom keeps up with the tide in politics and graver thought. It is only when he returns and tries to pick up the threads of English life again that he realises how far he has fallen behind the times. I am not speaking of those whose good fortune it is to be able to run home for a trip every two or three years, and so polish themselves up, but of the less happily situated, who do their six and seven, and even more, years in the country without a change. I did nine years once on a stretch, and confess to an utterly "lost" feeling when I first returned to England. For one gets, in the phrase of the East, "jungly," and that is far worse than ordinary provincialism. And then, again, after these prolonged absences there are so many changes in others as well as in yourself. Not till you return "home" and visit your old haunts and old friends do you realise how many faces are missing, and that those partings on the outward-bound steamer, when you were so full of excitement and anticipation of your new life, in the Golden East, had in them the finality of death-bed partings. Nor is it only faces that change; friends change, old familiar landmarks change, and feelings change. There is often a grievous disappointment in store for the returned Anglo-Indian, and I have frequently heard him sigh, "Home is not home!"

And that is a sad note to strike, for, as I began by saying, the Anglo-Indian's dearest word is "Home." To our cousins in the Colonies, the land they live in is home, and England only "the old country"; but to the Anglo-Indian, India is never anything but a place of exile, and when he returns to the scenes so fondly remembered, only to find that he has been forgotten, and to feel himself—as so many have done—a stranger in a strange land: well, you may score that down as a big debit item in the *pros* and *cons* columns we are considering! And I think I may say that home-sickness is the commonest complaint in India, cheerfully borne in the general, but always twinging. In the monotony of life, and its loneliness and lassitude, the thoughts fly back to England with a feeling Mr. Kipling has finely described in one of his earlier poems:

> "Give me back one day in England, for it's Spring in England now!"

I do not doubt that there come many seasons when the Anglo-Indian would willingly barter a month of his life for a single day in England. There is an overpowering sadness which steals over a man at times, and the exile casts his eyes over his surroundings, and ponders upon the vicissitudes of life and health and the spirit of the Land of Regrets enters into his soul!

And I think it is here you must strike your balance between the *pros* and *cons* of Anglo-Indian life. You will find no difficulty in arriving at a conclusion. Ask the Anglo-Indian at any period of his career what he would most like, and he will answer you, "To be going home." That is the glad cry of the East—going home! And its gladness is the best commentary on Anglo-Indian life!

INDEX

18